Historical Association of Ireland
Life and Times Series, No. 9

William Martin Murphy

THOMAS MORRISSEY, S. J.

Published for the
HISTORICAL ASSOCIATION OF IRELAND
By Dundalgan Press Ltd

First published 1997
ISBN 0-85221-132-5

© Thomas Morrissey, S. J. 1997
Cover design: Jarlath Hayes
Cover illustration: Leo Whelan, R.H.A., after the original by
Sir William Orpen, courtesy of Gerald Murphy
Frontispiece: 'The Demon of Death' in *Irish Worker,* 6 September 1913
Historical Association of Ireland, Dublin
Printed by Dundalgan Press, Dundalk

WILLIAM MARTIN MURPHY

'The Demon of Death spread his wings on the blast,
And spat on the face of the poor as he passed.'

— From Byron (slightly altered)

FOREWORD

This series of short biographical studies published by the Historical Association of Ireland is designed to place the lives of leading historical figures against the background of new research on the problems and conditions of their times. These studies should be particularly helpful to students preparing for Leaving Certificate, G.C.E. Advanced Level and undergraduate history examinations, while also appealing to the general public.

CIARAN BRADY
EUGENE J. DOYLE
Historical Association of Ireland

PREFACE

In undertaking this brief work, I have been encouraged by trade unionist friends, and apart from the special contribution of Gerald Murphy, mentioned in the Introduction, much assistance has been provided by David Sheehy of the Dublin Diocesan Archives, the staffs of the National Library and National Archives, and the observations of benign catalyst, Patrick Daly. Finally, I am indebted to Dr Fergus D'Arcy of University College, Dublin, who read the original, rather scattered manuscript at a very busy period for himself, and to Dr Ciaran Brady for his painstaking editing of the present text. Needless to say, any faults and failings which remain in the work are due to the limitations of the author, and of time.

THOMAS MORRISSEY, S. J.
Sandford Lodge, Ranelagh

CONTENTS

CHRONOLOGY OF MURPHY'S LIFE AND TIMES

1845   6 Jan.: William Martin Murphy born near Castletownbere, County Cork, only child of Denis Murphy, building contractor, and Mary Anne Martin.

1846   Family and business move to Bantry, County Cork.

1849   Death of Mary Anne Murphy.

c. 1851 Attends National School, Bantry.

1858–63 Attends Belvedere College, Dublin.

1863–4   Student of architecture, Dublin. Death of Denis Murphy. Returns home to run family business.

1867–75 Moves business to Cork city. Involved in light rail construction and in work for St Vincent de Paul Society. Marries Mary Julia Lombard.

1875–   Moves headquarters to Dublin. Develops interests in railways and tramways in conjunction with father-in-law, James F. Lombard, and in Clery's department store and the Imperial Hotel.

1885   Elected M.P. for St Patrick's Division, Dublin.

1886   June: defeat of first Home Rule Bill.

1890   Dec.: split in Irish Party; McCarthy replaces Parnell as chairman.

1891   Murphy funds *National Press*. 6 Oct.: death of Parnell.

1892   General election: Murphy defeated in St Patrick's Division by Parnellite candidate.

1893   Sept.: defeat of second Home Rule Bill.

1895   Murphy, backed by Healy, unsuccessfully stands in South Kerry by-election, in opposition to official Irish Party candidate.

1896   Involved in buying *Nation* newspaper. Commences Electric Tramway System in Dublin.

1900   Buys the *Irish Independent*. General election: Murphy defeated in North Mayo by Irish Party candidate.

1907   Organises Irish International Exhibition. Refuses knighthood.

1911–14 Vice-president, then president, Dublin Chamber of Commerce. Opposes Home Rule Bill as inadequate. Refuses support for Hugh Lane Art Gallery. Leads employers during great strike / lock-out.

1916   Apr.–May: Murphy's property destroyed in the Easter Rising, but he was unaware of *Independent*'s implied call for execution of James Connolly.

1

1916–18 Murphy takes strong stand against partition. Meetings with Lloyd George. Role in National Convention. Wages vigorous newspaper campaign against conscription.

1919   26 June: death of William Martin Murphy.

INTRODUCTION

This short work marks a step towards filling a notable gap in Irish historical biography. William Martin Murphy has been almost exclusively represented as a philistine and heartless capitalist who starved the workers of Dublin and their families into submission in 1913 and hounded James Connolly to his death in 1916. These aspects are re-examined here, but so too is Murphy's career as a good employer, as an international contractor of railways and light rail, an international financier, a press baron who revolutionised the Irish newspaper industry, and a fearless patriot who helped bring down the Irish Party and defeat conscription and, so it seemed at his death, prevent partition.

Despite so much prominent activity, Murphy remained a very private man. He left scarcely any personal papers. His great-grandson, Gerald Murphy, has been at pains to collect material on the family background, which includes the recollections of William's son, William Lombard Murphy, and a host of newspaper references, all of which he has generously made available. Other sources availed of in researching this biography are mentioned in the Select Bibliography.

The result of the research is a fuller and more complex picture of Murphy than has been conveyed by many social historians, but one which yet remains somehow two-dimensional. In this respect, Murphy still preserves much of the privacy and reserve that characterised his very public life.

1

EARLY YEARS, 1845–63

William Martin Murphy was born in Derrymihan, just east of Castletownbere, on 6 January 1845. The only child of Denis Murphy, a rising building contractor, and Mary Anne Martin, he was little more than a year old when his father moved his business to Bantry, and less than five years old when his mother died at the early age of twenty-eight. His grandmother, Mary Murphy (née Downey), now came to occupy a central place in the Murphy household and in young William's emotional life. His affection for her was reflected in many later reminiscences. She died, however, just five years later, in 1854. Such losses, intensified in the case of an only child, doubtless contributed to marked features in his later life—his self-reliance, a carapace of seeming imperturbability, and an aloneness that found fulfilment in hard work.

The years immediately following William's grandmother's death must have been difficult for both father and son, but presumably there was a housekeeper, and kindly neighbours like the celebrated Sullivan family gave advice and support. Denis Murphy was a close friend of A. M. Sullivan and T. D. Sullivan, who helped to run the weekly national and literary paper, the *Nation*. The upsets at home, however, did not seem to affect adversely William's performance at school. He attended the National School at Bantry, where he received a solid grounding in English and mathematics and is reputed to have contended for first place with a Richard Sheehan, who subsequently became Catholic Bishop of Waterford.[1] For further education it was customary for reasonably well-off families living in country areas to send their sons to boarding school. This was what Denis Murphy planned for his son, with the further intention that he proceed to qualify as an architect and thereby benefit the family business. Denis's close friend A. M. Sullivan advised, however, that William attend Belvedere College, Dublin, a day school, and stay in lodgings on the South Circular Road with two of the Sullivan boys, Donal and Richard.

The experience of leaving home to live in the big city remained etched in his memory to the end of his life. 'My earliest recollection of being thrown on my own resources', he wrote more than fifty years later, 'was when I left my home in the west of Cork . . . on a bracing March morning.' Significantly, he recalled with particular relish how, on the forty-mile coach journey from Bantry to Cork, he had shown scant 'respect for the age and rank' of a Captain Walker who put pressure on him to surrender his place of honour on the box seat alongside Mick Sullivan, a 'whip' of local fame.[2]

When William entered Belvedere College, after the Easter holidays in 1858, he was just short of his fourteenth birthday. He later recalled experiencing some bullying on his first day at class from a boy sitting near him. He sought at first to ignore it, but 'on receiving a more severe assault' he reached out and gave his tormentor 'a back-hander across the face'. He feared that expulsion could follow 'such a crime committed in the presence of the highest authority'. To his great relief, however, he heard his teacher, Father Murphy, who was also rector, say: 'That's right. He deserved that. I was watching him.'

As at most Jesuit schools then, a boy's fitness for a particular class was measured by his knowledge of Latin and Greek. And as young William, on his own admission, 'knew nothing, or next to nothing, of either', he had to join the junior class of the school on his arrival. Fortunately for him, his teacher, the same Father Murphy, took an interest in him. Noting that William was far more advanced in English than the other pupils, he dispensed him from English studies, and instead put him in a desk near himself and personally coached him in the elements of the classical languages. The effect of this helping hand was that Wiliam improved so markedly that after the summer holidays he was moved up two classes. Even more than in English, he had received a thorough grounding in mathematics in his National School, with the result that he won a first mathematical prize in Belvedere the year after he had entered. This, in turn, gave him entry to the natural philosophy class, which included chemistry and experimental physics which he enjoyed. He did not shine, however, at public speaking. As he represented it, 'I was always too self-conscious and diffident when I had to stand alone before an audience. This is a feeling I never got over.'[3] What he may have lacked in imaginative qualities, however, he made up in analytical powers, showing early signs of what was later described as 'his wonderful power for seizing the essentials of every question, and dealing with them clearly and vigorously'.[4]

There is scant record of student activities in those years. William and the Sullivans appear to have spent much of their free time in the offices of the *Nation* newspaper, and William attributed his subsequent involvement in the newspaper business to the interest generated there. Although he was very much his own master outside of school hours, this did not induce him to slacken off in his studies. His ambition and competitive instinct kept him attentive. 'I worked hard—very hard—to hold the head of my class, which whenever I became at all slack in my studies I had to yield to a rival.'

Overall he was thankful that he was sent to stay in lodgings in Dublin rather than to a boarding school. 'I gained a knowledge of the world and a reliance on myself at an early age', he observed, 'which I could not have acquired at a boarding school.' These benefits, he added, were of 'inestimable value when, little more than eighteen years of age, I lost my father . . . and had to take up the responsibilities of the business in which he was engaged'.[5] William went from Belvedere to work under the well-known Dublin architect, John J. Lyons. Concurrently he attended lectures at the Catholic University, and also devoted time to sub-editing and otherwise working for the well-established paper the *Irish Builder*, which his mentor, Lyons, owned and edited. He also at this time continued to work for A. M. Sullivan on the *Nation*.

Following the sudden death of Denis Murphy in 1863, of an illness contracted while overseeing the rebuilding of the Catholic church at Sneem for the third Earl of Dunraven,[6] William, at the age of eighteen, found himself called upon to run his father's extensive business. This involved not only church buildings but also many contracts for public works, a number of which were still in hand. Once again, members of the Sullivan family came to his assistance. Many years afterwards he wrote to the widow of A. M.

Sullivan that he had often thought that his success in life 'was largely due to the happy inspiration of A.M.' in getting his father to send him as a schoolboy to Dublin; and, he added, 'I have never forgotten A.M.'s night journey to Bantry the day after my father was buried, when, as a forlorn boy, he gave me counsel and encouragement at the most critical period of my life.'[7]

2

EXPANDING A BUSINESS; TRAMWAYS AND LIGHT RAIL; POLITICAL INTERESTS, 1863–90

I

Murphy never looked back. He had probably an acquaintance already with the sawmills and his father's contracting business. He now turned all his considerable ability and great energy to obtaining a thorough grasp of every aspect of the enterprise; and he went out of his way to build up a close, personal relationship with his workforce.

With the success of the business came the raising of horizons. Some time around 1867 he moved to Cork city, and some eight years later transferred his headquarters to Dublin. His business ambitions, however, did not blind him to the condition of the poorer population. While in Cork he was a prominent figure in the Society of St Vincent de Paul, and after his move to Dublin he established a conference of the society at Terenure and acted as its president for many years, and also involved himself in unostentatious work for many charities.[1] He was, by all accounts, a deeply religious man and a daily attender at mass.[2]

Murphy's business success, joined to his good looks, his assured yet unassuming manner, his religious observance and temperate lifestyle, made him an attractive marriage prospect. He married into one of Cork's old and distinguished families—a circumstance which further enhanced his business opportunities. His wife, Mary Julia Lombard, was the daughter of James Fitzgerald Lombard, whose business interests were wide-ranging. Irrespective of such assistance, however, Murphy's own solvency before he settled in Dublin was such that on arrival he became the owner of an imposing dwelling-house and extensive property running down to the River Dodder at Dartry. This new possession encouraged him to add horticulture and arboriculture to his hobbies, and to develop prowess with the axe in the style popularised by Gladstone.

8

Murphy was well prepared in other ways for a successful career in the capital. Conscious of the philistine image associated with 'business', he read widely in history, and to a lesser degree in literature, as well as in engineering and law, and could converse knowledgeably on many subjects. Moreover, he had a range of social contacts which eased the way for him. Apart from the extensive business links of his father-in-law, there were the numerous contacts of the Sullivans, the friendship of his former mentor, Lyons, the support of former Belvederians, and the links which he and his father had established with diocesan clergy and the religious orders, and with landlords like Dunraven. Soon after his arrival in Dublin, indeed, he enterprisingly availed of Sullivan contacts to offer his services to a virtually bankrupt committee established to erect a statue of Henry Grattan in College Green. He obtained, at a low price, a flawed but adequate granite base for the statue, thereby ensuring that the committee had money in the bank to complete the project.[3] It was an auspicious start.

Before long Murphy's attention was drawn to a development associated with an American, George Francis Train, namely the laying of rails in the public streets on which horses could draw large vehicles called tramway cars. The process minimised friction and road wear-and-tear and made city traffic much quicker and more convenient. Train had first tried the method in the United States, and then in Britain, and had plans in the 1860s to build lines in Dublin. These were not implemented; but in 1871 the firm of Barrington & Jeffers had proposals for a tramway service approved by parliament. By 1877 there were three tramway companies: the Dublin Tramway Company, the North Dublin Tramway Company, and the more recent Dublin Central Tramway Company. The last of these proposed to build various lines, several of them in competition with the Dublin Tramway Company. This new company was able to build these lines quickly and economically by means of Murphy's building business, which was very much to his benefit, as he and James Fitzgerald Lombard were both directors of the company.

In 1880 all these tramways were amalgamated in the Dublin United Tramways Company,[4] under a board chaired by Lombard. Murphy was a director, and became chairman and guiding spirit from 1899 until his death in 1919. It was a profitable undertaking.

The tramway system in Dublin was electrified after 1896. This encouraged skilled and white-collar workers to move to the suburbs, for the tramways tended to follow housing development, and so the usage of trams expanded almost continuously. Murphy would comment years later: 'I made the Inchicore line, and promoted and made the Harold's Cross, Clonskeagh, and Palmerston Park lines',[5] and an English visitor, Arnold Wright, observed in 1914 that 'nowhere in the United Kingdom can you find a service which is so thoroughly comprehensive in its routes or so convenient in every respect as a passenger-carrying agency'. 'No important part of the city and its spreading suburbs was left outside the range' of the service. 'From a point under the shadow of the Nelson Column in Sackville Street, in the very heart of the city', Wright concluded, 'you can go to most of the outlying districts, while a skilfully devised system of cross routes enable you to get from one area to an adjacent one expeditiously and with a minimum of resistance.'[6] The profitability of the enterprise was such that for many years it 'paid a dividend of 6 per cent on both its £10 preference shares and its ordinary shares'.[7] Standing under the shadow of the Nelson Pillar in Sackville Street in 1914, Wright could not avoid a sense of Murphy's commercial strength as he witnessed the trams converging and then, looking down towards the river, saw further evidence of his wealth in the Metropole Hotel on the right and Clery's large department store on the left side of the street.

Murphy's involvement with tramways was but part of a wider interest in light railways generally, which he had initially seen as offering him scope as a contractor. There had been a steady growth in Irish railways from 1850 to 1880. Remote districts were opened up, towns were brought within hours of Dublin rather than days, labourers had money to spend, and the transport of goods and export opportunities were enhanced. The government viewed the development of the railways as essential to the development of the economy, and by means of loans through the Public Works Loan Commissions and the Board of Works provided inducements to contractors. Very conscious of this, Murphy used his local contacts, and his reputation for competence, to secure the contract for the Bantry rail extension, from Drimoleague to Bantry, which was formally opened on 3 July 1881.[8] In the following year, with a blend of audacity, enterprise and goodwill, he prevailed on the Archbishop of Dublin, Cardinal McCabe, as a director of the Cork and Bandon Railway Company, to sign a paper appointing 'William M. Murphy, of Dartry, Rathmines' to be proxy in his absence at a meeting of the directors of the company to be held on 15 July 1882 and 'to vote in his name upon any matter related to the undertaking . . . in such manner as he . . . doth think proper'.[9] Thus, at thirty-seven years of age, William Murphy was beginning to be a familiar figure among railway proprietors in the country. By this time, too, he was a man with a family. By 1882 there were five sons to his marriage.

Much of his time in these middle years was devoted to political life and to the development of his railway interests. In 1885 he was elected to parliament for the St Patrick's Division, Dublin City, and continued as the Nationalist member for the division until 1892. T. P. O'Connor remarked in his *Memoirs* that Murphy's presence in parliament proved 'useful to him from a commercial point of view', as the fortunes of tramways and railways 'depended largely on the sanction of parliament'.[10] O'Connor, however, was a hostile critic where Murphy was concerned. The latter, as has been seen, was already active, well before his election, in the construction of light railways (taking that very general term to refer to railways where the rails, sleepers and so forth were merely required to be adequate to bear a weight no greater than eight tons with respect to any one pair of wheels,[11] and whereon the speed of trains was restricted). As well as the Bantry extension in 1881, he completed the Clara–Banagher railway in 1884. The construction of Irish railways was rendered attractive by low labour costs and the relative absence of tunnels and viaducts, as well as by the government incentives.

No doubt Murphy's experience in parliament encouraged him to become an authority on the law relating to railways, and this was of importance in respect of the complicated series of acts from 1883 to 1891 which provided assistance for the construction of light railways in the western and congested districts of Ireland. Thus, under the Public Works Loans Tramways (Ireland) Act, 1886, which authorised the Treasury to lend money on the deposit of guaranteed shares, he managed to obtain a loan of £54,000 for the West Clare Railway, of which he was chairman-proprietor as well as contractor. He completed work on the West Clare as far as Miltown Malbay in July 1887. Further incentives for the building of light railways were provided by Arthur Balfour's Railway Acts of 1889 and 1891, and he also availed of these. Money was granted by parliament for the construction of specific lines, provided these were sponsored by existing railway companies. Of the thirteen lines constructed under the 1889 act, two, the Bantry Bay extension of 1892 and the Skibbereen and Baltimore railway of the following year, were constructed by Murphy and worked by the Cork, Bandon and South Coast Railway, of which he was a director.[12] Other constructions of his were the Mitchelstown to Fermoy line, which opened in March 1891, the South Clare line which followed in August 1892, and the Tuam to Claremorris railway, opening in April 1894. At that point he turned his attention to plans for the introduction of an electric tramway system in Dublin, and he did not return to railway construction until 1906, when the Wexford–Rosslare line was completed. It was his final such work in Ireland.

In addition to construction work, his role of proxy for Cardinal McCabe indicated how keen he was to make his way on to the boards of railway companies. Again he succeeded. The 'Irish Railway Half-Yearly Reports' for the six months ending 30 June 1885 show 'William M. Murphy, J.P., Dublin' as a director of the Cork and Bandon Railway Company, the receipts of which were described as 'satisfactory . . . considering the continued commercial depression'.[13] The reports for the half-year ending 31 December 1885 indicate additional advancement, noting that 'William Martin Murphy, Esq., J.P., a gentleman of considerable railway experience, has been elected to fill the vacancy caused by the retirement of Patrick Martin, Esq., Q.C.' on the board of directors of the Waterford and Limerick Railway.[14] Linked in with the Waterford and Limerick line, but independent of it, were the West Clare and the South Clare Railways, of which, as noted, he was also director. The years before 1914 have been called the 'golden years' of the Irish railways. They may have been so for the main lines, but few of the light railways paid their way. Not surprisingly, from the closing years of the nineteenth century most of the many privately owned rail companies, over thirty-four of them, began to be absorbed into a few larger units in the face of competition. As might be expected, Murphy availed of this trend. The Waterford–Limerick line expanded into the Waterford, Limerick and Western Railway, and that was amalgamated into the Great Southern and Western Railway to foil the British Fishguard Company's plans to buy up the Irish lines converging on Waterford. The Great Southern and Western, indeed, became a formidable consolidation, for it formed an alliance with the British Great Western Railway, which had considerable influence at Fishguard, and this opened opportunities for entry into Fishguard and the British rail system.

At the amalgamation of the Waterford, Limerick and Western into the Great Southern and Western Railway in 1901, Murphy did not immediately obtain a place on the Great Southern board. The report for the half-year ending 31 December 1903, however, recorded that on the death of the deputy chairman, Colonel Sir Gerald R. Deese, 'the vacancy had been filled by the election of Mr William Martin Murphy, who has had large experience in the construction and management of railways'. That he was 'elected' says much for his reputation as a director, since the great majority of the directors were Protestants with strong Unionist sympathies. His close involvement in the operation of railway companies continued almost to the end of his life. In 1911–12, indeed, the Irish Railway Reports indicated that he was not just a director of the Great Southern and Western Railway, and of the Cork–Bandon Company, but was also chairman of the West Clare Company, the South Clare Railway, and of the Athenry and Tuam extension to Claremorris.

II

The fact that Murphy may have availed of his political position and connections to further his business is not to suggest that he entered political life purely out of self-interest. He came from a very politically conscious background where the sense of patriotism was strong and where it was widely believed that prosperity for Ireland could only come about through Home Rule. Alexander Sullivan, K.C., later commented that in addition to the Sullivans, there came to the imperial parliament from the shores of Bantry Bay the three Healys, the two Harringtons, James Gilhooly, and finally William Martin Murphy. And he added: 'Willie Murphy was left some means at the death of his father, but not much. The great fortune that he acquired was the creation of his own brain and enterprise. Prosperity never spoiled him.' He remained 'an unaffected West Cork man . . . the devoted friend and worshipper of my father, whose children always addressed him as "Uncle Willie" '.[15] Coming from that background, Murphy was proud of being Irish and conscious of being what was then a rare species, a highly successful Irish Catholic businessman. As part of that pride there was a sense of social responsibility. Thus, at a public meeting under the auspices of the National Labourers' Dwellings and Sanitary Association, reported in the *Freeman's Journal* on 30 December 1889, he pointed out that he was able to provide dwellings for his employees at 'most modest rents' and that, with the facilities available, 'there was no excuse for the large employers of labour in not providing suitable dwellings for their employees'. In the same vein, he asserted the importance of ploughing profits back into the country instead of earning idle interest abroad, and of providing large-scale employment; and he had the reputation of being a fair, if demanding, employer.

Something of this outlook was conveyed, less than two years after his election as a member of Parnell's Home Rule Party, in a lecture on 'The Irish Industrial Question' at the Wood Quay National Registration Club on 10 January 1887. Emphasising that for the country to advance in material prosperity a national government was necessary, he pointed to the example of Belgium and what had been accomplished in Ireland under Grattan's parliament. English penal legislation, he observed, had left the Irish at home with a sense of insecurity and hopelessness, which might be rectified by the settlement of the land question. As to the alleged absence of capital in Ireland, the fund of capital available in the Irish people should not be forgotten. 'At the present moment', he claimed, 'I am able to get on a length of 20 miles of railway as many as a thousand men, most of whom are either small farmers or their sons, who . . . but for this exceptional employment, would be altogether idle for one half of the year, and nearly so for the other half.' If such men had security of tenure, and education suited to the wants of the people, not much more in the way of capital would be needed to enable them to be profitably employed.[16]

Then moving on to points relating to his personal experience and concerning which he had strong views, Murphy commenced with the principle that as there was 'a great amount of labour in the country . . . no effort should be spared to find remunerative employment for it', and that any man who could 'make two workers to be employed where one was employed before' would 'have done a thing deserving of credit'. Among Irish businessmen there was now a far more hopeful and positive view of industry than among their English counterparts. But it was sometimes stated that 'the difficulty of dealing with workmen' was an obstacle to setting up industry in Ireland. He did not deny that there were difficulties between employers and workers, but these existed in other countries and did not prevent trade flourishing. He did deny, however, that unrest was all the fault of workers, or that workers in Ireland were more difficult to deal with than workers elsewhere. 'My own experience extending over 20 years', he asserted, 'is that by meeting men fairly and by treating them as possessing equal rights, I have never failed to make reasonable and amicable arrangements.'[17]

Much of the problem lay with the employers themselves. Many of the manufacturing businesses had failed because they stayed in old grooves and failed to introduce 'the best processes and the newest appliances'. And a persistent cause of decline among once flourishing industries, he added vehemently, was the 'snobbishness and toadyism of men, and the sons of men', who had made money in trade, but now saw trade as 'not respectable' and aped the 'idle class that lived upon the land' for which 'they toiled not'. Three years later, indeed, he was to underline the unreality of employers. Regarding the building labourers' strike in Dublin in 1890, he wrote to the *Freeman's Journal* on 24 March pointing out that the master builders had no case. The labourers were seeking only 4d an hour, which would come to an average of 18s a week all the year round, which was what he, Murphy, as a contractor had been paying as the going rate ten years previously. Subsequently he was invited by the union secretary to chair the public meeting announcing the arbitration settlement, at which, together with the arbitrators, Archbishop William Walsh, Michael Davitt and Charles Dawson, he was loudly cheered by the assembled workers.

But if he was critical of employers, this did not mean that he absolved workers from all blame. Hence in his 1887 address he reminded workers that 'they must help the employer to compete in the market with his goods', otherwise both of them would go to the wall. 'They must be more sober and more diligent; and . . . while insisting that they shall have all fair play, they must sometimes put themselves in their employer's place, and see whether they are allowing him a margin to pay for his plant, and capital, and expenses, without which the shop must ultimately close.' And strongly conscious of management's duty to manage, he warned that 'the right of combination' was 'a powerful weapon' and should be used with 'consideration and prudence'; and Irish workers should keep in mind that their interests and those of their counterparts in England were often not identical. At the same time, he emphasised that when Irish people were told that 'the great obstacle to Irish prosperity' was their love 'for politics and for agitation', they should keep in mind that 'whatever rights our people possess were won by agitation.'[18]

Murphy's conclusion reflected his active identification with the politics of Parnell, and his close links with Parnell's able assistant, T. M. Healy, a fellow Bantry man and married to a Sullivan. Shortly after his own election as a member of parliament Murphy's loyalty to his Bantry kinsman was put to the test. At the start of February 1886 Healy had found to his dismay that Parnell was supporting Captain O'Shea's candidature for election in Galway, even though the Irish Party had nominated a local man, Michael Lynch, for the position. Healy insisted on following the normal procedure. Prompted by Parnell, T. P. O'Connor rallied support for O'Shea and obtained signatures from prominent members of the party and sent telegams to others. One of these, sent to Murphy on 8 February, stated: 'Parnell has intimated to us his leadership at stake in Galway contest. Healy's speech has created impression that party generally is against Parnell. Will you authorise us to attach your name with ours to public declaration upholding Parnell? Awaiting reply. Wire. T. P. O'Connor, Sexton, Esmonde, Leamy, T. P. Gill, T. Harrington, Wm O'Brien.'[19]

Murphy refused. As always, he had a strong dislike of being put under pressure; and, besides, an unfortunate experience of Parnell's meanness and high-handedness in not acknowledging trouble and expenditure undertaken on his behalf predisposed him to support Healy.[20]

O'Connor's rallying of many of the senior members of the Irish Party placed Healy under a cloud. The latter's combative and venomous wit did nothing to ease the tension. Murphy, as a junior member of courteous demeanour, lost no ground. O'Connor, who was so critical of him later, remarked of this period: 'Mr Murphy and I had been fairly good friends in the earlier days. He was a man, indeed, with whom it was rather hard to be at enmity in the ordinary intercourse of life.' O'Connor went on to describe him as 'a thin man, with alert movements', a tranquil face, and 'an entire absence of the angry vituperation in which Irishmen usually expressed their feelings'. He seemed to go through life 'with unbroken temper and inflexible equanimity' and 'also had the other great quality of inflexible courage'.[21] Elsewhere in his *Memoirs* O'Connor added to this pen-picture by remarking that Murphy 'had perfect control over himself, was a spare eater and practically a teetotaller', and 'his indomitable will and his extraordinary tenacity of purpose made him, though he very rarely spoke, one of the men on whose words and acts the fate of the party depended'.[22] The blend of these characteristics, together with his standing as the local M.P., and the fact that he had been highly regarded by Cardinal McCabe, drew the cardinal's formidable successor to him.

3

MURPHY, ARCHBISHOP WALSH AND THE PARNELL SPLIT, 1890–1900

I

Archbishop William Walsh was known for his strong nationalist sympathies, and in his early years as metropolitan of Dublin was, with Archbishop Croke of Cashel, an influential supporter of the Irish Parliamentary Party led by Parnell. He had played a part, indeed, in discrediting the forged letters published by *The Times* in 1887 to undermine the character of Parnell and the reputation of the Irish national movement. Walsh also kept abreast of developments at Westminister through his local member of parliament, Murphy, and some other Irish members. During 1889 Murphy and Walsh exchanged letters with reference to government legislation regarding hospitals and education, but the main interchange of correspondence commenced the following year, subsequent to the filing of a divorce suit against Parnell and Gladstone's call, on 24 November 1890, for Parnell's retirement from the leadership of the Irish Party for the sake of Home Rule. When Parnell declined, the majority of the party felt it necessary to requisition a meeting to consider the question of his leadership, and the bishops found themselves under pressure to make a public pronouncement.

Murphy telegraphed Archbishop Walsh on 26 November that there was no one on hand 'strong enough to insist upon the only course that could avert a catastrophe', namely Parnell's resignation, and he requested the archbishop to make a statement.[1] Walsh replied that the Irish members of parliament should 'take time', and that they had 'no mandate from the country that would authorise them to wreck the movement', and he urged 'calm, full deliberation'.[2] Subsequently Murphy sent a long letter on the situation to Walsh and followed it with a telegram stating that the archbishop's letter had been 'construed in Parnell's favour by many people', and that some members thought it right to acquaint him of this, as he might 'desire to dispel misapprehension'.[3] However, the archbishop was not ready to commit himself.

Meanwhile, on 29 November, Parnell issued a manifesto in the *Freeman's Journal* which, avoiding all mention of the divorce, accused his opponents in the party of being seduced by the offer of a very meagre Home Rule Bill from the Liberal Party, and that for this miserable offer the Irish people were being asked to throw over their leader at the bidding of an English politician. He thus shifted emphasis from the moral to the political plane, and appealed above the heads of the politicians to the people at large. It was a calculated exercise in misdirection on the basis of misinformation.

Severe pressure to speak out was immediately experienced by the Catholic hierarchy. Archbishop Walsh sent an urgent telegram to Murphy on the evening of the manifesto's publication. It ran:

> Strong telegram from Archbishop of Cashel to vice-chairman [Justin McCarthy] urging Parnell's retirement. See it at once, see also detailed interview of mine *Central News* tomorrow's papers. Standing committee of bishops meets on Wednesday to consider our position if present leader is retained. We have been slow to act, trusting party will act manfully.[4]

On receiving this telegram, Murphy telegraphed back at 5.20 p.m. that same day, 30 November: 'Have no fear about the result. Large majority, probably two to one—if vote challenged at all. Some of the proverbial rats already in motion.'[5] That evening he expanded his telegram into a letter. He had been satisfied from the issue of Gladstone's letter, that 'there was a majority of the party who would remove Parnell from the chairmanship'. At the party's meeting on the following day, however, no one knew whether or not Parnell would 'cut up rough'. Murphy believed he would not, but would 'either retire, giving way to the inevitable, or withdraw and refuse to recognise our action'. Most of the men supporting Parnell believed it would be better that he retire, but nevertheless would not vote against him.[6]

Archbishop Walsh's interview with the representative of the Central News Agency in Dublin was published on Monday 1 December. He finally made his position quite clear: 'If the Irish leader would not, or could not, give a public assurance that his honour was unsullied, the party that takes him as a leader can no longer count on the support of the bishops of Ireland.' He was confining himself, he said, 'almost exclusively to the moral aspect of the case'.[7]

At the party's meeting, the historic Committee Room 15 meeting in the House of Commons on 1 December, Murphy's predictions were shown to be misjudged. Parnell mustered 27 supporters and showed no sign of giving way or withdrawing, but instead occupied the chair, arbitrarily accepting and rejecting what motions he pleased. On Wednesday 3 December the standing committee of the bishops met, and afterwards Archbishop Walsh, as chairman, sent a telegram to Justin McCarthy, the vice-chairman of the party, informing him that it was important that he and the party members know of the bishops' 'unqualified pronouncement' that 'Mr Parnell [was] unfit for leadership, first of all on moral grounds—social and personal discredit as a result of divorce court proceedings—also in view of inevitable disruption, with defeat at elections, wreck of Home Rule hopes, and sacrifice of tenants' interests'.[8]

As the party's deliberations dragged on, Parnell seemed, despite the pronouncements of the bishops, no nearer being deposed on Thursday than he had been on Monday. Walsh, in a letter to Murphy, indicated that the 'country was rising rapidly in opposition to continuance of Mr Parnell's leadership of the party', and that instances of contradictions in Parnell's statements made it impossible 'to put any faith whatever in his word, in public or in private'. He asked: 'Why not think and act boldly ? The party, I fear, will otherwise be led into some morass.' A postscript requested him to show the letter to Sexton, Healy 'and any one or two others you think desirable'.[9]

On the following day, Saturday 6 December, with the meeting still grinding on relentlessly, Murphy sent a number of communications to the archbishop. At 4.30 p.m. he wrote: 'Our party of 44 are as solid as one man for no more compromise. You have no conception of the indecent and unscrupulous tactics adopted by Parnell.' Murphy added that he was glad that the efforts at compromise had fallen through. His reasons for saying so indicated the extent of the change that had taken place in a short time:

If we can succeed in getting rid of this man and reconstituting the party, Ireland will have escaped from one of the greatest dangers with which she was ever threatened. While acknowledging his enormous services in bringing the question to its present position, if we got Home Rule with his power unimpaired we should be only exchanging British parliamentary rule for the autocracy of a man who has proved himself to be filled with some of the worst passions of human nature.[10]

At 5.24 p.m. he sent a telegram to Walsh: 'Have just withdrawn in a body, forty five . . . McCarthy having come over. We meet to elect chairman and committee.'[11] Finally, later that evening, he added to the letter written at 4.30 p.m.: 'Parnell will "cut up" very badly, I'm sure. Will hold on to the funds and otherwise endeavour to destroy the Irish cause: for he knows he can no longer serve it.'[12]

The split in the parliamentary party soon widened into a countrywide division as each side hastened to publicise their case. The urgency to achieve effective communication was rendered more immediate by Parnell's decision to challenge the chosen party candidate for the by-election scheduled for North Kilkenny on 22 December. In this predicament, Murphy, with his interest in and experience of the newspaper business, his power of organisation and his financial strength, came to occupy a leading role.

It seemed an almost impossible task at first. The control of the party's funds was in Parnell's hands, as he and his close supporter, Dr J. E. Kenny, were two of the three trustees of the £50,000 on deposit with an American banking firm in Paris. He had the support of the most influential newspaper in Ireland, the *Freeman's Journal*. And where the public was concerned, his name and reputation had an almost magical appeal. Moreover, he was a shrewd tactician, who also now showed himself a fiercely passionate man able to join rhetoric to resolute action. On 10 December, the morning after his return to Dublin, he and his followers seized the offices of the nationalist weekly, *United Ireland*; and next morning at breakfast, learning that the majority party had reoccupied the offices, Parnell led a group of his followers to the premises and, crowbar in hand, personally smashed down the door, scattered his opponents, garrisoned the premises like a fortress, and proclaimed that 'What Dublin says today, Ireland will

say tomorrow.'[13] Within two weeks Parnell had further consolidat-
ed his power by capturing and purging the National League, the
Irish Party's political machine.

Meanwhile, as Parnell's opponents, soon known as the
'Patriotic Party', tried to co-ordinate their efforts, the bishops and
priests promoted opposition to him. Politics and religion had
become intermeshed. The already bitter divisions were intensified. Archbishop Walsh advised Murphy regarding publicity. On 8
December Murphy returned to Ireland and, after four days of
hectic work and the additional turmoil caused by the seizure of
the party's newspaper, reported to Walsh that an 'emergency
paper' would come out on 15 December under the name of
Suppressed United Ireland. 'We purpose', he continued, 'sending a
circular to all priests and secretaries of branches of the National
League in Ireland stating that, the central offices having been
captured by Mr Parnell, we request they will communicate with us
with a view to reconstituting the central organisation.' He was at
work on a prospectus for a new morning paper. 'We have a good
deal of lee way to make up,' he concluded, 'but when we get our
little daily organised I think we shall be "before the world"
again.'[14]

Following an interchange of letters with Archbishop Walsh
relating to the prospectus and to the method of financing the new
paper, Murphy reported on 17 December that 'the emerging
paper' was coming out under many difficulties and that £5 shares
were being issued.[15] An undated letter around this time added
that the paper would be brought out at the *Nation* offices and that
his own office at 39 Dame Street would serve as temporary party
headquarters. He also suggested bringing out from the *Nation*
office 'a daily bulletin during the crisis to be called "the Patriotic
Party" or some such name', which would, he thought, sell largely
in Dublin for a halfpenny 'and could be sent *gratis* for distribution
in Kilkenny and elsewhere'. He would also help to put up a
fund.[16] The strenuous election campaign in Kilkenny proved
successful for the majority Irish Party, the Parnellite candidate
being defeated by 1,165 votes. That evening, 22 December,
Murphy, in Dublin, chaired the first general meeting of the
National Committee, which had been established at his office in
Dame Street and which planned to replace the National League,

which had been taken over by the Parnellites. Murphy claimed that the committee had been joined already by some 3,000 prominent citizens.[17] The next day, 23 December, he wrote to Archbishop Walsh that the meeting had been excellent and that 'with the news of the Kilkenny election the proceedings were enthusiastic'.[18] The conduct of the election, however, had created a chasm. The Parnellites, with reason, railed at the vicious and intemperate language used at times by members of the clergy, and at their domineering interference in the political arena; while Cardinal Manning of Westminster, who followed Irish affairs with great interest, was of the view, on the other hand, that the Kilkenny election had shown 'that Mr Parnell and his friends would if they could shut up the bishops and the priests in the sacristy as in France'.[19]

Walsh, writing to Murphy, charged that not enough was being done in building a strong local organisation. 'I entirely agree', Murphy responded on 27 December, 'as to the need of extending and perfecting the organisation of the National Committee.' But their path in Dublin would be easier if they had the 'presence and countenance of the clergy', and 'it should not be forgotten', he added trenchantly, 'that it was barely a fortnight since we got home from London until Christmas day arrived, and that we had to face the situation with the national organisation and the national press in Dublin opposed to us. Since then, we have created a new organisation, started and kept going a daily paper, arranged for the establishment of a new morning paper' at a time when 'nearly all our forces' were 'away during the time fighting the Kilkenny election'. 'Moreover,' Murphy observed, even more pointedly, 'the work was carried on without subscribed funds. I advanced the whole expenditure so far myself.'[20]

The support of the *Freeman's Journal* was a decisive factor in prolonging Parnell's struggle. Murphy, Healy and others produced first a limited paper with the title the *Insuppressible*, rather than Murphy's original suggestion, the *Suppressed United Ireland*, and thereafter a more substantial paper styled the *National Press*. Healy and Murphy were among the directors, and the former devoted himself entirely for three months to getting out the new journal. It was a difficult task to gain advertisers and support in Dublin, which was intensely Parnellite, partly owing to the influence of the *Freeman*. An explosion which damaged the *National Press* premises testified to the local hostility. Eventually, with the financial backing of Murphy and the support of the bishops, advertising poured in; and a prominent Irish Party figure, Thomas Sexton, M.P., agreed to act as editor. By 6 March 1891 the paper was ready to run, with an envisaged printing of 60,000 copies for the first issue.[21] It was the beginning of the end for the Parnellite cause. In the *National Press*, on 22 April, Murphy expressed dismay at Parnell's impenitence—brazening out with 'indecent affrontry' a gross offence against the highest social as well as religious laws. And Healy, meanwhile, used the journal to give vent to a range of relentless and personal attacks, a form of journalism also reflected in the *Irish Catholic* under William F. Dennehy.

At the same time, Murphy and other prominent members had been active in raising a fund for the party, and in organising a national convention of the branches of their newly organised party machine. In June 1891 Healy informed his father: 'We find William Murphy a true man—most serviceable, level-headed and able.'[22] Earlier, in April, the Parnellites lost a second and even more crucial by-election (in North Sligo), and then in August, thanks to the pressure of the bishops, supported now by John Dillon and William O'Brien, recently released from jail after completing their sentence for agrarian agitation, the *Freeman's Journal* abandoned Parnell.[23] The latter struggled on, nevertheless, and set about launching a new paper, the *Irish Daily Independent*, but died before it was published. His funeral was immensely imposing. In defiance of the dissuasion of many priests, some 100,000 people attended as the cortège slowly wound its way from Dublin's City Hall to Glasnevin cemetery, to the solemn strains of the 'Dead March' from *Saul*. The conflict, and Parnell's early death, left a legacy of intense bitterness and mistrust.

Murphy himself was a victim of the conflict. His political constituency, St Patrick's Division, was avidly Parnellite. He paid the price of opposition. At the general election in July 1892 he received as the Irish Party candidate only 1,110 votes, compared with 3,694 votes for the Parnellite, William Field, who was to remain the constituency representative for many years. Moreover, given that the Dublin working class as a whole remained intensely loyal to the memory of the 'martyred Chief', and were increasingly vocal in demanding general workers' rights, Murphy came to be depicted among them as the unscrupulous betrayer and destroyer of Parnell, and, in time, corresponding terms came to be applied to him as an employer and capitalist. But even within the ranks of those who opposed Parnell, Murphy found himself faced with hostility and misrepresentation in the immediate wake of the leader's passing. For the aura of division generated by the struggle between Parnellites and the majority of the party soon found expression also among the majority members themselves.

II

With Parnell's passing, the almost chemical antagonism between John Dillon and Tim Healy, which Parnell had held in check, and which had been kept submerged during the challenge to his leadership, now came openly to the surface. The two men were very different and irritated each other. Dillon, sober, unbending, taking himself and his political lineage very seriously, presented an irresistible challenge to the mercurial Healy, whose emotions lay near the surface and who could not resist the witty, irreverent and often wounding remark.

Murphy's and Healy's control of the *National Press* placed them in a position of power which Dillon and O'Brien determined to challenge. The *Freeman*'s abandonment of Parnell gave them the opening they sought. Arguing in the committee of the party that there was no longer need for two major dailies speaking for the party, they proposed that the *National Press* be amalgamated with the *Freeman's Journal*. Healy, who had invested so much time in the *National Press,* and Murphy, who had invested money as well as time, strongly opposed the proposal. At length after a struggle, they gave way and counselled the shareholders of the *National Press* to transfer to the *Freeman*. The upshot was that those shareholders held a third of the shares after amalgamation, and were represented on the board of the *Freeman* by Healy, Murphy and a Joseph Mooney. Dillon, assisted by Thomas Sexton, now set out to gain control of the *Freeman* board, and in the process to squeeze out Healy and his close associates. Neither side, so soon after the Parnell crisis, wished to appear in public disagreement with the other. Sexton and Dillon seem to have played on this, using the threat of resignation more than once to achieve their ends. If carried out, it would have advertised a split.

Annoyed and frustrated, Murphy protested to Archbishop Walsh on 9 April 1892 against 'giving these men anything like the influence they are seeking'.[24] Disagreements on the board continued into 1893, until, after Healy's and Murphy's departure from a meeting, and without any prior notice, Dillon proposed Sexton as chairman of the board. The board members elected him, despite the protests of Mooney that it was irregular.[25] Subsequently, writing to the archbishop and aware of the latter's wish for a commercially orientated board rather than the current politically weighted one,[26] Dillon asserted that Murphy and Healy had taken up 'an utterly irreconcilable attitude'—refusing to consent to any scheme of reconstruction which involved their retirement from the board. Yet five days later Dillon had to inform Walsh that Murphy had seconded a resolution requesting him, Walsh, to act as arbitrator, and offering the resignation of *all* the board members. Dillon concluded: 'You are now in a position to save the company from the ruin which threatened. Whatever decision you arrive [at], all the members of the board are pledged to accept it and carry it through.'[27]

Walsh realised he was being manipulated by both sides and soon determined to withdraw, but then, on 24 January 1893, allowed himself be persuaded to continue by Dillon and Sexton. He agreed to complete a report within a month. By 20 February he had done so, and then asked to meet with the board to discuss the carrying out of his recommendations. The board named Monday 6 March for the meeting. On that very day the archbishop received letters from Messrs Murphy, Healy and Mooney, stating that they would not regard his decisions as binding on them.[28] It had come to their ears, it seems, that they were likely to be replaced on the board by people acceptable to Dillon, but unlikely to be acceptable to the shareholders of the former *National Press*. Their action was viewed by the archbishop as a breach of faith, and subsequently he was less than friendly towards Murphy and Healy. Within a few years the latter was restored to favour, but Walsh's relations with Murphy seem to have remained strained, and correspondence between them was formal and confined to necessary interchanges.

The conflict on the board continued. Dillon was implacable in his opposition, representing to the archbishop that it was 'essential' that no partisan of Murphy be left on the board, because if there was a man left to back him, he would never cease to give trouble, and with 'his extraordinary gift for intrigue' might succeed in gaining ascendancy.[29] Murphy eventually suffered the loss of money and position; but worse was to follow. The *Freeman* controversy was waged in a limited arena; it was followed by one which was fought in the full glare of publicity. Murphy had lost his seat in Dublin. In September 1895, subsequent to the general election of that year, a by-election arose in South Kerry. The Irish Party in the region, led by the local clergy, came out in support of Murphy as candidate—whether with or without his connivance is not clear. The party's central committee, led by Dillon, challenged the choice, summoned a special convention, and put up as their candidate a London Irishman, T. G. Farrell, who had been chosen by T. P. O'Connor. Murphy was presented as the choice of an unofficial convention and hence as a challenge to party unity. Supported by Healy, Murphy determined to stand. Both candidates stood, and with Healy on one side and William O'Brien on the other, the contest produced a harvest of invective. At the end of it all, Murphy was well beaten: obtaining a mere 474 votes to 1,209 for his opponent.[30]

Following up this victory, Dillon and his supporters proceeded with what Healy termed their 'vendetta'. The first steps were taken by T. P. O'Connor, who had Healy formally expelled from the Irish National League of Great Britain on 7 November. A week later, after a long debate, Healy, Arthur O'Connor, William Murphy and two other prominent Healyites were expelled from another central nationalist body, the council of the Irish National Federation, by 48 votes to 41, the reason given being their independent stand at the South Kerry by-election. On the following day, at a private meeting of the parliamentary party, Healy was expelled from its executive committee, though he remained a member of the party. Three months later, on 11 February 1896, Justin McCarthy resigned from the chairmanship of the party, and on the 18th Dillon was elected in his place.

Before long Dillon abolished the committee and conducted the party's affairs very much in the manner of Parnell, taking advice only from a small group, of whom the chief were William O'Brien, T. P. O'Connor, Edward Blake and Michael Davitt.[31]

Dillon's control both of the party and of the *Freeman* led to unease and criticism among a number of nationalists. The *Irish Catholic* in March 1896 launched a series of vitriolic attacks against him. Murphy, meanwhile, prepared his own means of attack. He was an honorary treasurer of an organisation entitled the People's Rights Association, which had links with the weekly *Nation* and wished to acquire a daily newspaper. They purchased the ailing *Nation* with a view to producing a daily edition. Murphy provided the greater part of the capital and gradually became the owner of the entire debenture capital of the Nation Company Ltd; there is little doubt that he viewed the paper as a means of getting even with Dillon for his expulsion from the *Freeman* board, his humiliating defeat in South Kerry, and his removal from the council of the Irish National Federation. The final years of the century, as a result, showed forth the extent of the divisions that beset the Irish Party. There were now three nationalist dailies: the *Freeman's Journal* controlled by Dillon, the *Daily Nation* controlled by Murphy, and the Parnellite *Independent* controlled by John Redmond.

The leadership of Dillon from 1896 to 1899 was scored by criticism. Healy, in the *Daily Nation*, turned his vinegar-tongued wit against Dillon and William O'Brien, and the latter in his *Irish People* in 1900 made the celebrated remark on 'the division of labour in the firm of Messrs Healy, Murphy and Co., Moral Assassins, now in course of liquidation: Mr Murphy bought the knives, and Mr Healy did the stabbing'.[32] His mention of 'liquidation' referred to a further newspaper venture on Murphy's part.

The Daily Independent was due for sale in the bankruptcy court. The *Freeman* made an offer for it. John Redmond wrote to Healy, with whom he had established friendly relations and who he knew would support him for the chairmanship of a united party. 'Is there any way', he asked, 'of saving the *Independent* from being sold to the *Freeman*? . . . For all our sakes, don't you think it would be wise for Murphy to step in now and offer to reconstruct the company, or buy ?'[33]

Murphy had already lost money on newspapers and saw little prospect of profit in the new venture; nevertheless, Healy persuaded him to step into the breach and foil the *Freeman*'s plans to purchase the paper. Murphy determined to exercise personally control the *Independent*'s policy.[34] Because of his ownership of all the debentures of the *Nation* company, he was in a position to take over all the copyrights and other assets and thereby amalgamate the *Daily Nation* with the *Daily Independent*. Moreover, as mortgagee in possession of the assets of the *Nation* company, he was to become in August 1900 owner of the copyright of the *Irish Catholic*, though the paper itself 'was not amalgamated with the *Independent* and remained all through an entirely separate publication under distinct editorial control' and Murphy claimed not to influence its policy.[35] Under Irish Independent Newspapers Ltd in 1901 there was included: the *Irish Daily Independent* and the *Daily Nation*, the *Weekly Independent* and the *Nation*, the *Evening Herald* and the *Saturday Herald*, together with company offices in Fleet Street, London, and in Cork, Belfast and Waterford, as well as in Trinity Street, Dublin.[36]

With the election of Redmond as leader of the Irish Party, there was a sense of new beginnings; and the lure of political position induced Murphy once again to allow his name to go forward for parliament. The opening was in North Mayo, and Murphy understood that his name would go unchallenged. Once more, however, O'Brien and Dillon foiled his hopes. He was chosen by the convention, but O'Brien and Dillon adopted a rival candidate, Conor O'Kelly. Murphy appealed to Redmond. 'If you would exercise your authority in these Irish contests,' he declared, 'a good deal of the bad blood which is being engendered would be avoided.'[37] Redmond did not intervene, and once more Murphy suffered defeat. The new leader, in Murphy's view, had shown himself a weak reed. And much later, during the fateful year 1916, he was to observe that 'Redmond's cardinal mistake as a leader was made soon after his election, when he failed to assert himself', probably not realising that the party 'wanted a leader even more than he wanted a following'. He allowed himself to fall under the domination of others, more particularly of what Murphy termed the triumvirate of O'Brien, Dillon and 'the immaculate T.P.'.[38] O'Brien was never forgiven by Murphy for his

part in the defeats in South Kerry and North Mayo, and years later, when Healy and O'Brien formed an alliance, Murphy remained obdurate and hostile, even to the extent of expressing quiet jubilation at an O'Brien electoral defeat.[39]
The Mayo disarray finally disillusioned Murphy with the Irish Party. What changed dissillusion into implacable hostility, however, was probably the party's opposition, under the direction of T. P. O'Connor, to a bill favouring Murphy's business interests. With the large electricity generating plant set up for his Dublin United Tramways Company,[40] and in view of his own engineering knowledge, Murphy considered that he was in a good position to run an efficient lighting system for the city of Dublin. The concession lay with the Dublin Corporation, but there were many complaints at its inefficiency. A new City of Dublin Electric Lighting Bill was being introduced in Murphy's favour. T. P. O'Connor, on his own account, took an active part in opposing it. He enlisted the support of Conservative members, especially those from Ulster, who were hostile to everything nationalist and were disposed to strike a blow at a corporation composed mainly of nationalists. Canvassing was used by both sides. Healy and the friends of Murphy canvassed widely over a number of weeks. They managed to get the bill through the committee of the House of Commons and succeeded in obtaining a strong representation of their cause. They were successful up to and including the second-last stage. Their majority, however, was by a mere thirteen votes. 'In the last stage of the Bill', as O'Connor expressed it, 'I was more successful, and it was rejected, and Mr Murphy and his company remained without the enormous addition to their power and their income.'[41] With remarkable obtuseness, O'Connor was to comment of Murphy that 'for some reason or other he had a sleepless and ruthless hatred of the Irish Party under Mr Redmond'.[42] Murphy would deny 'hatred', but his onslaught was to be both intense and relentless, and the machine that rendered him something of a nemesis for the party was the *Daily Independent*, which he started so hesitantly in 1900 at Redmond's suggestion.

4

ELECTRIC TRAMWAYS, INDEPENDENT NEWSPAPERS AND CHARGES OF PHILISTINISM, 1895–1913

I

In 1895, following his election defeat and ejection from the board of the *Freeman,* Murphy returned to less contentious, more profitable ventures. He travelled to the United States to learn of developments in the area of street traction by elecricity, and returned home an authority on the subject. In 1896 he proposed its introduction in Dublin on an overhead wire and trolley system. It was the first such venture in Ireland or Britain.[1] The project proceeded, despite opposition from contemporary environmentalists to the unsightly overhead wires, and within twenty years the Dublin United Tramways Company was to control 100 miles of line and was reputed to provide one of the most efficient services in the world. Both its fees to the public and its remuneration of its workforce appear to have been comparable to tramway services in Britain, and the company, moreover, provided housing accommodation at moderate rentals for many of its traffic men[2] and operated its own factory, at Inchicore, Dublin, where its cars were built and repaired.

The company's great overall success owed much to Murphy's energy, power of organisation, specialised knowledge and grasp of detail; and this attracted attention far afield. Hence, in addition to being contractor of the Dublin system, he became a promoter and contractor of electric tramways in Cork, Belfast, the southern district of London, in Ramsgate and Margate, Bournemouth and Poole, Hastings and district, Paisley and the Isle of Thanet. In those years also he completed the construction of his last light railway in Ireland, the Wexford–Rosslare line (1906). And from his offices in Dublin and London, when past his sixtieth year, he carried out successfully the construction of a section of railway in the Gold Coast Colony in Africa, one of the first railway contracts

31

to be entrusted by the crown colony government to a private contractor. Even the Argentine capital, Buenos Aires, owed its first tram tracks to him. Healy's friend P. A. Chance, seeking to characterise, perhaps even caricature, Murphy in those years, commented that he went through life with the Companies Act in one hand and the *Imitation of Christ* in the other.[3]

While this multifarious expansion was mushrooming in the first decade of the twentieth century, Independent Newspapers developed into a major enterprise. Murphy's first years with the *Daily Independent* were marked by financial loss, much as had been his experience with the *Daily Nation*. And politically now there was little to achieve, as he and his associates had been expelled from the Irish Party in 1902. By 1904 Murphy was ready to move out of the newspaper business, even though a revolutionary concept had emerged in London in the form of a halfpenny paper, the *Daily Mail*, established by Alfred Harmsworth, Lord Northcliffe, a native of Chapelizod, Dublin, who then went on to another startling success with the new *Daily Express*. But after consulting Northcliffe,[4] and having obtained further expert advice, Murphy decided to follow Northcliffe's example. Consequently, in late July 1904 Murphy ordered two new printing machines from the Goss Company in Chicago, and proceeded to purchase linotype machines, establish new modern printing offices in Middle Abbey Street, and take on new staff.[5] He appointed another Castletownbere man, Tim Harrington, the news editor of the *Irish Daily Independent*,[6] to the position of editor to the new paper, the *Irish Independent*. Modernisation included having many photographs, a major innovation at the time, and the extensive use by reporters of the recent invention, the telephone. Like the successful *Daily Mail* and *Daily Express*, the *Irish Independent* was to be a non-partisan newspaper.[7]

Murphy announced that his new-look paper would be published on 2 January 1905. It seemed like an impossible target. There was less than three months in which to reconstruct the premises to house newspaper offices and printing-presses. And meanwhile the new Goss printing-presses, then the most up-to-date available, which were ordered in late August, had to be completed, tested by the manufacturers, dispatched, installed and thoroughly tested in Dublin before the end of December, a task which, in normal circumstances, would have taken much longer than the four months he had allotted. To add to all the pressure, the landlord of the offices at Trinity Street decided to eject the *Daily Independent* before the Middle Abbey Street offices were ready. Murphy appealed to his friend, John Clancy, Sheriff of Dublin, who managed to have the ejectment put back until the end of December. Up to the last fortnight of December 1904 the editorial staffs of the *Irish Daily Independent* worked out of Trinity Street, while the printing staff commenced work in Middle Abbey Street. The first of the new Goss machines arrived. It was installed and tested by the end of December, but by itself it did not have enough capacity to print the new newspaper. The second Goss arrived late, only days before the launch. The mechanical engineer, Tom`Stobie, and his staff worked wonders, remaining on duty for the entire week before the first publication, some of them not leaving the building during that time. Then at 2.35 a.m. on 2 January 1905, the printing-presses began to turn. Some 50,000 papers were printed and circulated that morning.[8]

The paper's first editorial announced that its aim was 'to make this journal what a modern newspaper should be—the "biography of a day", brightly written and attractively presented, free from unwholesome sensationalism' and presenting the news of the day 'without colouring or prejudice'. The *Irish Independent*, it was promised, would be 'independent in fact as well as in its name', free from partisanship in its editorial columns, and although 'uncompromising in its support for the restoration of the national rights of Ireland', it would 'be found acceptable by every class and creed'.[9]

A high-flown start indeed. Among the unusual features of the publication were signed articles written by known political and literary contributors, a bright magazine page for women readers, a serial story designed to have readers look forward to the next issue, and a special sporting feature which catered for the growing interst in sport. And the photographs, of course, added greatly to the paper's attractiveness. The first six issues ran a competition for readers to choose the best advertisement, prizes being offered for advertisers as well as for the winning entries. The emphasis on attractive advertising paid off. The use of five different typefaces showed advertisers what could be done to present their goods and services in the best light, and how inadequate by comparison was the cramped newspaper advertisement of the past. The cheap price of the paper at a halfpenny favoured circulation, which within a short time was three times that of any other journal in Ireland, and this was a further inducement to advertisers to pay the higher rate demanded by the *Independent* for advertisements.

There was much criticism of the large sums of money Murphy poured into the paper with seemingly little assurance of a profitable return. He replied disarmingly that he was happy to spend money in pursuit of a hobby. In fact his expenditure was closely calculated, and 'for the first two or three years' of the new *Independent* 'he devoted a great deal of his time and attention to the actual management'. After the first few years of personal supervision, assured that the paper was secure financially, he left the further development largely in the hands of its manager, editor and staff. In 1910, recalling the start of the enterprise, he pointed out that he had accomplished the development of the new *Independent* within the budget he had set himself, adding complacently: 'For such an undertaking, compared to other similar properties, £50,000 is a very small capital indeed.'[10]

By 1910, moreover, Independent Newspapers Ltd (incorporated on 31 December 1904), under his active management, included the *Evening Herald*, which became the first evening paper to pass a daily sale of 100,000 copies, and the *Sunday Independent*, Ireland's first Sunday paper, which was to more than double its circulation from 21,000 copies in its first year, 1907, to 55,000 in 1912. Part of the secret of the volume of sales was the system of distribution. Where previously the Dublin papers did not arrive until the afternoon in country towns, or cities, and so presented no competition to local daily papers, the *Independent* started arriving in the morning and so increased its own sales at the expense of the local journals.[11] And Murphy introduced a further practice which other newspapers felt obliged to follow, namely the publication of an auditor's certificate of the paper's circulation; this recorded not just the gross circulation, which gave the number of copies sent out to newsagents without any indication of how many copies were returned unsold, but the net daily sales, that is actual sales after free copies and unsold or spoiled copies were deducted. By late 1915 the *Irish Independent* was said to have a circulation of 100,000 and to be making £15,000 a year; three years later it was making £40,000.[12] The paper won praise from friend and foe alike for its production. Tim Healy described it as a new portent which had flamed into the Irish political sky. The reference to the 'political' sky suggested that Murphy's strongly proclaimed ideas of impartiality and absence of political prejudice had faded once the financial future of the *Independent* was assured. T. P. O'Connor, as indicated earlier, made no bones about this. 'There was not a day', he claimed, in which the *Independent* 'did not contain some open or subtle and quiet attack on the Irish Party'; but as an experienced and, indeed, creative newspaperman himself, he had to acknowledge the great source of its influence—'its cheapness, its brightness, and its venom got it innumerable readers, even among those who hated it most'. Hence, he concluded, 'of all the many agencies that finally broke down the Irish Party, and led to the regime of Sinn Féin and its accompaniments, the . . . *Independent* and William Murphy behind it must be regarded as perhaps the most potent'.[13]

Although T.P. was far from being an unbiased witness, there is no doubt about the *Independent*'s hostility to the Irish Party. 'The paper owes them nothing but ill will,' Murphy reminded Harrington on 23 October 1910.[14] In Tim Healy's often reiterated view, however, Murphy held Harrington in too high esteem, was too loath to intervene in editorials, and could not control his editor.[15] Nevertheless, it is clear that Murphy did intervene from time to time on issues of particular interest to him, and was then likely to send notes and comments, enclose letters or articles from friends, request that a favourite leader-writer be set to work on his suggestions, and specify parliamentary figures and policies to be supported or attacked.[16] Still, his interventions appear to have been spasmodic until the threat of partition loomed in 1914. Then he became actively involved. In the following year, indeed, Harrington was to demand an assurance that he would not force his 'unpopular politic views' on him 'with a view to getting them into the editorial columns of the *Independent*', and he declared 'rather heatedly' that he was 'sick and tired' of acting as a buffer between Murphy and his paper.[17] Murphy, nevertheless, appears to have continued to intervene frequently from 1914 on. An indication of this was reflected in a passing remark of the editor some months after the Easter Rising. The *Independent* was pressing for the release of Sinn Féin prisoners. Murphy's son protested to the editor against the paper's Sinn Féin sympathies—only to receive the blunt response from Harrington that no man could serve two masters![18] Indeed, from comments made by Healy to his brother Maurice, it appears that Murphy himself by early 1917 was writing editorials against partition and in favour of full Dominion Home Rule.[19]

II

It has to be kept in mind that while the newspaper developments were taking place Murphy was also engaged not only in the development of tramways and railways outside Ireland, but also in supervising the operation of the Imperial Hotel and Clery's department store in Dublin, and in chairing or otherwise officiating on the boards of railways and of other organisations in Ireland, professional and voluntary. One such organisation was the Dublin Chamber of Commerce.

To get on in business in Dublin it was essential to be a member of the Chamber. Murphy was elected a member as early as 1876, and by 1906 his social and business standing was such that he was co-opted onto the central council[20] of what was still a predominantly Protestant and Unionist body. Subsequently, as will be seen, he became vice-president and president, but even as early as the year 1907 his position on the council, his ownership of the *Independent* and his financial reputation brought him unaccustomed publicity. The *Independent* put forward the idea of an Irish International Exhibition, and Murphy was asked to chair the Finance and General Purposes Committee set up to examine the proposal. The exhibition was intended to be international in scope, while also seeking to provide a window on Ireland and on its industries. Soon it became evident that the exhibition was going to be a success, and that the main credit lay with the organising energy and urbanity of Murphy. Almost inevitably, denigrators made themselves heard. It was alleged that he was acting out of self-interest, that King Edward VII was likely to attend the exhibition, and that Murphy expected to be knighted for his work. Stung in pride and independence, he made it publicly known that he would not accept a title if one were offered.

The Irish International Exhibition was a great success, though not without its moment of near farce. Held in Herbert Park, Ballsbridge, it attracted an estimated 2,750,000 visitors, including Edward VII. The latter arrived with a schedule which included the public knighting of William Martin Murphy after the royal speech. Murphy had made it clear to the viceroy, Lord Aberdeen, that he would not under any circumstances accept a knighthood. Aberdeen neglected to pass on the information, and on the day, as Murphy remained adamant, and as the king called for the ceremonial sword, the viceroy found himself obliged to step forward to state that this portion of the proceedings was being omitted. Outwardly His Majesty preserved his calm. Later that day Murphy, fearing that his motives might be misconstrued, sent Aberdeen a formal letter for the king, not wishing, as he put it, that His Majesty 'should leave Ireland thinking that he had left one churlish man behind'.[21] His letter assured the monarch that he did not refuse the honour on political grounds, and that as a constitutional nationalist he accepted a common crown for both countries, and he expressed his personal respect for the present sovereign. On the following day at Leopardstown races Aberdeen handed the letter to the still discomfited king, who responded with a message that he quite appreciated the writer's position.[22] Officially that was the end of the matter, but Dublin gossip gleefully elaborated on the story for many weeks.

Murphy was 'a most regular attendant' at meetings of the central council of the Dublin Chamber of Commerce and gained the reputation of being 'always foremost in looking after the interests of the commercial community'.[23] In 1911 he was elected vice-chairman of the Chamber, and arising from that was appointed deputy chairman of the 'large and representative committee' established to organise events and decorate the city to a greater extent than ever before to honour the visit of the king and queen; and Murphy and the honorary secretary, Sir William Fry, presented an address to the sovereign on behalf of the Chamber.[24] During his time as president Murphy figured promi-

nently on many social occasions, including at a meting of the
Association of Chambers of Commerce of the United Kingdom
and British Chambers in Foreign Countries, held at the Hotel
Metropole, London, from 12 to 14 March 1912.[25]
The minutes of the central council of the D.C.C. are preoccu-
pied with day-to-day events and have surprisingly little to say about
Murphy's presidency in relation to the strike and lock-out of 1913,
but there is no doubt that what the Dublin Chamber came to
value above all about Murphy was what after his death it termed
'his services to employers during the years 1911 and 1913, when
he successfully fought syndicalism'. Those services, the council
continued, 'will never be forgotten'. Certainly his role in the
struggle against 'syndicalism', as they understood it, was never
forgotten—though not predominantly in the laudatory manner
hailed by the council, but rather as portrayed by Jim Larkin's
press and by the pens of literary figures such as W. B. Yeats and
George W. Russell (AE).

The negative perceptions of Murphy first came to the fore
with his opposition to Parnell, and were carried forward by the
pervasive propaganda of the Irish Party machine from the turn of
the century. In 1907 these perceptions received impetus with the
charge of calculated place-seeking by his political enemies, and
the further accusation of heartless philistinism from certain
members of Dublin's literati because his *Independent* newspapers
had joined in the widespread criticism of aspects of Synge's
Playboy of the Western World as a slur on the Irish people.[26] Six years
later the perceptions hardened and widened when Larkin's
relentless propaganda portrayed him as a ruthless exploiter of
workers and their families, and some of Dublin's artistic
community found further grounds of criticism in his opposition
to a plan for an art gallery to house a collection of modern
French painting offered to the city of Dublin by Sir Hugh Lane.
There were numerous opponents of the project, but Murphy
became a scapegoat for the opposition of many. In fact, despite
the charges of philistinism, the issue appears to have been not so
much the quality of the art or its appreciation, but the impractical
nature of the plans presented for the gallery and the actual
handful of people who were pressing for it.

Sir Edwin Lutyens, who was comissioned to draw a design for

the project, produced one for a building spanning the River Liffey. The money required to realise this ambitious dream depended on the munificence of rich men such as Lord Ardilaun of the Guinness family and William Murphy. They declined to make substantial contributions, Murphy proclaiming bluntly that the need for such an extravagant building had not been demonstrated[27] and that a 'handful of dilettante' were promoting a project 'for which there is no popular demand and one which will never be of the smallest use to the common people of this city'.[28]

On 12 August 1913, moreover, the council of the Dublin Chamber of Commerce, at a special meeting, protested strongly 'against the erection of any structure other than a vehicular bridge over the River Liffey'. They sent a copy of their resolution to the Lord Mayor, the City Clerk and to the Port and Docks Board. At the meeting Edward H. Andrews, presenting the motion, pointed out that Murphy had spoken in a personal capacity, but that he, Andrews, wished the Dublin Chamber to object to this unsatisfactory structure as a distortion of the visual appearance of the river, as involving considerable maintenance cost owing to the dampness of the river and its possible deleterious effect on the paintings, and also because there were alternative sites available, and there were proposals for a great central thoroughfare to pass at, or close by, the proposed site for the art gallery.[29] The plan was finally rejected by a vote of the Corporation. Murphy's personal opposition, and the fact that he was president of the Dublin Chamber of Commerce and owner of the *Independent*, which had been outspoken against the plan, encouraged Yeats and a number of others of the literary and artistic community to lay the main blame on him for Hugh Lane's subsequent angry decision to withdraw his offer to the city.[30]

Yeats was particularly effective in creating an unsavoury image for posterity. Murphy for him was the very symbol of the rising, rapacious, bourgeois Catholics who were not only supplanting the Protestant ascendancy, but had destroyed his hero, Parnell, had brought the insensitive Catholic clergy forward as a force into Irish politics, and had spurned the dramatic genius of Synge and rejected Lane's offer of a superb art collection. Murphy and his kind, moreover, were placed in contrast to Yeats's other romantic heroes, the Fenian John O'Leary, recently deceased, and all those who had given their lives without counting the cost. Yeats brought all together in his poem 'September 1913', which, despite its title, was in no way concerned with the great strike and the suffering of worker families;[31] yet its first stanza was seen as an attack on Murphy in that context, and characterised him for ever as Yeats saw him:

> What need you, being come to sense,
> But fumble in a greasy till
> And add the halfpence to the pence
> And prayer to shivering prayer, until
> You have dried the marrow from the bone?
> For men were born to pray and save:
> Romantic Ireland's dead and gone,
> It's with O'Leary in the grave.

Such opposition, however, left Murphy, to all appearances, unmoved. He carried on, refusing to be diverted from what he considered to be right. Outwardly, as Healy observed after the dark election defeat of 1900, he behaved 'like an Indian at the stake. He never blenches or complains.'[32] The major crisis, however, which tested him above all others, and which discredited him most of all in the public perception, demands special consideration.

LABOUR AND THE EMPLOYERS, 1907–14

I

William Martin Murphy prided himself on his good relations with his workforce, and especially the skilled trades. His support for the building labourers in their strike in 1890 has been noted, and two years later in the intense election against the Parnellite Nationalist, William Field, support for Murphy, as an advocate of painters' rights, was urged by John Ward, president of the Metropolitan House Painters' Trade Union and former president of the Dublin Trades Council.[1] The minutes of the latter body, indeed, show instances of tributes to him; and on the occasion of the first Irish Trades Union Congress he made a token donation to their hospitality fund and provided the delegates with free passes on the Dublin tramway system.

There was an almost inevitable tension, however, between Murphy's desire to control and operate a prosperous business and his wish to be a just and caring employer. At times the tension slackened and the capitalist side prevailed. This may be seen, for example, in his relations with the tramway men. In 1890 they formed a union, but it collapsed seven years later because Murphy refused to recognise the union or to grant the men a nine-hour working day. Refounded in 1901, it collapsed again in 1904 when he refused to yield on the issue of working hours. In 1906 there was an attack on the Tramways Company at the Dublin Trades Council, not with regard to working conditions but because of the importation of tramways from Britain; but even then, George Leahy, a plasterer and a former president of Congress and of the Dublin Trades Council, spoke up to deprecate what he considered were 'personal attacks against Mr Murphy'.

In that year, 1906, the passing of the Trade Disputes Act proved a turning-point for trades unions. Thereafter union officials were immune from liability for damages when they acted in contemplation or furtherance of a trade dispute; acts of tort (right of action for damages) against unions were prohibited; and peaceful picketing was permitted. Unions, as a result, were free to conduct a militant campaign for the rights of members without fear of prosecution. One of the first to take advantage of this new situation was the Liverpool-born Irishman, Jim Larkin, who in 1907, acting for the National Union of Dock Labourers, established branches in Derry, Belfast, Newry, Dundalk and Drogheda. In 1908 Larkin was involved in the carters' strike in Dublin, in the course of which other parts of the workforce were encouraged to come out in sympathetic strike with the carters. Despite attacks on him as the tool 'of an English labour union' inflicting misery on thousands of Dublin artisans,[2] Larkin managed to bring out 3,000 men and persuaded them to hold firm for some time, even though he had hardly any funds to support them. The executive of his union, however, had become tired of his independent and maverick ways. They refused assistance and dismissed him, despite his obvious powers of leadership.

Following his dismissal, Larkin set up an Irish general workers' body, the Irish Transport and General Workers' Union. He was its first general secretary. Almost immediately he involved his new union in militant action. In 1909 the I.T.G.W.U. initiated a strike at the Cork docks, which spread to the Cork Steampacket Line and to the Great Southern and Western Railway. The employers responded by forming a federation which agreed to dismiss anyone who 'wilfully disobeyed any lawful order out of sympathy with any strike or trade dispute', and they further agreed that no member of the federation would employ any man who had been discharged. Financially secure, the employers prolonged the dispute deliberately, refusing all efforts at mediation. Some seven weeks after the start, the strike collapsed. The example of the Cork employers was not lost on their Dublin counterparts, and it was particularly instructive for Murphy, who knew the Cork scene well and was himself on the board of the Great Southern and Western Railway. Larkin, moreover, experienced some immediate after-effects. He was charged with defrauding the dockers by taking subscriptions for a non-existent branch of the National Union of Dock Labourers and making promises of benefits which could not be delivered. On 17 June 1910 he was found guilty. Typically, he had kept no accounts. He was sentenced to twelve months' imprisonment with hard labour.

There was an outcry. The sentence was quite disproportionate, and Larkin's popularity rose. Released after a little more than three months' incarceration, he emerged, in the eyes of the labouring population, as a martyr and messiah, and he used his powerful platform presence and compelling rhetoric to play the combined roles to the full. He and his supporters gained control of the Dublin Trades Council. In 1910 he proposed the foundation of an Irish Labour Party; and the fears of employers were further accentuated that year by the return from North America of James Connolly expounding a radical form of syndicalism.[3] Connolly strengthened the workers' cause, though he personally experienced Larkin as 'singularly unreliable' and a bully.[4]

In May 1911 Larkin produced his own newspaper, the *Irish Worker and People's Advocate*. By December, according to union sources, some 95,000 copies were being sold. It was even more abusive, tendentious and prone to character assassination than the other main 'minority papers' in the city, Arthur Griffith's *Sinn Féin* and D. P. Moran's *The Leader*. At the same time, it provided a practical service in exposing employers of child labour and factories which were sweat shops, and in providing workers with information on their legal rights.

The summer of that year, 1911, was marked by a fever of unrest. A brushmakers' strike was followed in June by an I.T.G.W.U.-organised walk-out in sympathy with the striking seamen and firemen in England. This was followed by a dockers' strike; and then, on 14 July, carters and fillers also went out in sympathy with the seamen and firemen—this in direct breach of an agreement they had made in 1908. On 20 July the Custom House docks were brought to a standstill when the men walked off without warning. The widespread disruption in Britain, which provoked much of the Dublin unrest, spread in August to the British railways. The Home Secretary, Winston Churchill, called out the troops, who fired on the strikers and evoked a nationwide rail strike which, coupled with the threat of imminent war with Germany, forced the government to capitulate.[5] The unions were given the promise of a royal commission to investigate the working of the conciliation boards established by act in 1907, and all workers were reinstated in return for an immediate return to work.

The demonstration of union power not only put additional pressure on employers, it also raised the expectations of workers and their trust in 'syndicalism', understood as the capture of power through a form of industrial action which made a calculated use of the sympathetic strike as a means towards a general strike. In this scheme of things, transport unions were in a position to play a key role by 'blacking' goods bound for, or coming from, firms in dispute with their employees. In Ireland the front line was occupied by the Amalgamated Society of Railway Servants (A.S.R.S.), which controlled the largest body of workers in the largest railway company, the Great Southern and Western Railway (G.S.W.R.); and, in the atmosphere of 1911, they were necessarily drawn to the exercise of the sympathetic strike as advocated and practised by the I.T.G.W.U.

From late August the I.T.G.W.U. was in dispute with a number of timber yards. The most prominent of these was Kelly's timber firm. On 15 September 1911 the dispute took on a new dimension. Two porters at a Great Southern and Western railway yard in Kingsbridge (Heuston) Station refused to handle a load of timber from Kelly's. A walk-out followed, the men declaring that they would only return to work when the company agreed not to handle 'tainted' goods. This was refused, because of the carrier obligations of railway companies. Similar incidents followed next day on the Midland and General Western Rail and the Great Northern Railway. By 18 September the strike was widespread in the Great Southern and Western Railway. This brought the executive of the A.S.R.S. to Dublin, where they endeavoured to institute negotiations with the rail companies. When their efforts failed, they called an all-Ireland railway strike to take effect on 20 September. Subsequently they extended the deadline by two days, without effect.

The strike threatened to paralyse the trade of the country. The council of the Dublin Chamber of Commerce met in special session on 21 September 'to consider the present crisis', and it 'determined to support by every means in its power the decision of those Irish railway companies which have observed their legal obligations'.[6] A week later, at a general meeting of the D.C.C., employers were exhorted to form an employers' organisation to face what one termed 'not a strike in the ordinary sense . . . but the beginning of a social war . . . in the sense of setting class against class'.[7] The G.S.W.R. strike, as a result, came to assume a special importance. How it was dealt with by the directors of the company was seen as critical for the future.

They determined to meet pressure with pressure. Murphy, as vice-president of the Dublin Chamber of Commerce, and with an eye to his own business interests, supported them in their unyielding determination. In response to the declaration of an all-Ireland strike, the directors replied with a week's notice of their intention to close the workshops with effect from 28 September, thereby putting an additional 1,600 men out of work. Moreover, they brought in labour from England to keep the line going, and even managed to acquire some locomotive men. Subsequently members of the Royal Engineers were brought in to man the engines. Only thirty-eight of the original drivers had remained at work, a testimony to the workers' determination. The new drivers, however, ensured that more and more trains ran, and this undermined the morale of the strikers. Their union, besides, had disappointed them by confining the strike to Ireland and not bringing out its members in England. On 27 September, the day before the threatened closure of the workshops, the strikers' representatives asked for a meeting with the G.S.W.R. board. At the meeting next day the company required that the men withdraw their demand concerning tainted or 'black' goods and express their regret for striking without notice. As to reinstatement, applications would have to be made by each man to the head of the respective department, and each would have to sign an undertaking to accept all traffic offered. The company reserved the right to re-employ. The directors, in the words of the uncompromising chairman, Sir William Goulding, were 'determined at any cost to re-man the system'.[8] On 2 October the company added further pressure. Two days later the workers' representatives accepted the company's terms.

Thus, within a very short time, despite the support of a major British union, the strikers, in Murphy's words, 'were beaten to the ropes'. The memory, and the process, stayed with him. The memory stayed too with the A.S.R.S. Indeed, a historian of the 1911 dispute has observed that the railway workers' disastrous experience in that year occasioned their subdued role during the

1913 labour troubles; while where the directors were concerned the main effect was 'confidence in their ability to resist trade unionism'.[9] The strike, moreover, led to the council of the D.C.C. finally deciding at their meeting on 27 September to nominate a small committee to open a subscription list with a view to forming an all-Ireland employer organisation 'which shall advise its members on labour troubles as they may arise and make effective preparations to protect the trade and commerce of the country'.[10] The establishment of this one big union or federation of employers in 1911 was to be of key significance when, under Murphy's leadership, employers decided in 1913 to take on Larkin's 'one big union'.

Triumphant after the railway dispute, some members of the Dublin Chamber of Commerce called for a special general meeting at which they proposed to censure the conduct of the government during the strike. At the meeting on 2 November the proposers compared the apathy of the government in the face of law-breaking and so-called 'peaceful picketing' with that of Churchill sending in the troops during the railway dispute in Britain. Significantly, Murphy dissented with unusual fluency and vehemence, unable on this occasion to conceal his impatience with the political and social insensitivity of some of his colleagues. Those proposing the motion, he observed bluntly, had not themselves suffered in any way from picketing, and he believed that a motion of censure passed by the Chamber would be seen as 'the action of a Unionist body attacking a Liberal administration', while 'to suggest that the government should have brought out an army to mow down peaceful picketers was neither possible nor thinkable'. The massacre of Peterloo was not likely to be repeated in their time. As to the reference to Churchill, 'there was no bloodshed in Ireland, no people shot down, as in England and Wales . . . no serious rioting'; hence to say 'that the government failed in their duty was a gross misrepresentation of the facts'. The motion was defeated.[11]

Murphy realised, like other prominent businessmen on the council of the Chamber, that there were stormy days ahead, and he did not wish to alienate the government. Already in 1911, indeed, Larkin had made an attempt to organise the tramway company, and Murphy was conscious that he would try again.

Consequently, as was his way, Murphy planned ahead. Speaking at the quarterly meeting of the Chamber of Commerce on 2 September 1913, he stated that he had not gone into that year's conflict 'in a light-hearted and haphazard way' and that 'no man could go into a fight like this unless he was prepared to take some trouble and lose some money'. His planning was assisted, he added dryly, by the fact that 'generally Mr Larkin was good enough to state in advance what he proposed doing'.[12] As he spoke on 2 September 1913 Murphy was expecting a short, intense, all-out operation which would quickly bring the strikers to their knees, as had happened in the Great Southern and Western dispute.

II

Murphy was laid low by a long, unexplained, but 'serious illness' from the beginning of March, or end of February, to the beginning of May 1913. It was occasioned in part, one suspects, by the additional demands on him as president of the Chamber of Commerce, particularly in the light of the inevitable forthcoming showdown with Larkin. He was almost sixty-eight years of age and, for all his outward imperturbability, was a worried man. Later he would emphasise that workers were at their strongest before a strike, but that once they struck they had fired their 'last cartridge' and the tension was lifted from the employer. Murphy took pains to mention that before 1913 he had never had experience of a strike, and that an employer in that situation, anticipating a strike, 'got terrorised'.[13]

In Murphy's case, the anticipation was all the more frightening in that Larkin was spewing forth a persistent stream of personalised invective against him and creating a caricature of him in workers' minds as a 'capitalist sweater', a 'whited sepulchre', or, as depicted in the *Irish Worker* of 7 September 1912, 'a creature who never hesitated to use the most foul and unscrupulous methods against any man, woman, or child, who in the opinion of William Martin Murphy stood in William Martin Murphy's way, a soulless, money-grubbing tyrant'.[14] Nevertheless, reacting as ever to personalised pressure or bullying, Murphy determined, six weeks after his return to work following his illness, to face down the union's threat. Conscious of renewed attempts to infiltrate the Tramways Company, he summoned a meeting of tramway workers after midnight on Saturday 19 July 1913. More than 700 men attended.

Murphy prepared his text very carefully in an attempt to create an atmosphere of trust and friendship, while at the same time making it clear from the start what the company's policy was in respect to the Irish Transport Union. He knew, he declared, that an attempt was being made to seduce men to go on strike, and he wished them to understand clearly that the directors of the company had 'not the smallest objection to the men forming a legitimate union' of their own, provided they did not ally themselves to 'a disreputable organisation' under 'an unscrupulous man' who sought to use them 'as tools to make him the labour dictator of Dublin'.

He was aware, Murphy continued, of those who were actively fomenting a strike. It would not take place, and if it did, it would prove 'the Waterloo of Mr Larkin'. He had given authority to the manager 'to summarily dismiss' any man who pushed for a strike within the tramway staff. He did not wish to preach against strikes in general—indeed, there were occasions when strikes were justified 'and ought to be carried out' if they had any chance of success. But few strikes were successful. The best illustration of this, he observed, was ' the great strike, twelve or eighteen months ago, on the Great Southern and Western Railway', when, even though the funds of the Amalgamated Society of Railway Servants of the United Kingdom were behind the strike, 'the men were beaten to the ropes in nineteen days and had to sue for peace'. There was, he claimed, even less chance of success against the Tramways Company, which would 'spend £100,000 or more to put down the terrorism which [was] being imported into the labour conditions of this city'.

Having thus issued his challenge and warning, Murphy moved to more benign and personal matters. In the fifty years since he became an employer of labour he had not only 'never experienced a strike', but had never had 'any serious friction' with his men, and this was because they knew that he 'had sympathy with them, helped them when they were in trouble, was always ready to meet them, not as a master to his servant, but as man to man (*applause*)'. Turning to the benefits of employment in the company, Murphy pointed to the demand for places, and how conditions and pay were more favourable than in other organisations. Recalling his own thirty-six years' association with the Dublin Tramways, he observed that in all that time he had had the most pleasant relations with the employees of the company, whom he respected 'as a fine body of men', and he flattered himself that they had a regard and respect for him. At his age, Murphy concluded, he could readily retire from his position, but he loved the work and, he added, 'I like to be associated as long as I can with an undertaking and with its men, of whom I am so proud (*applause*)'.[15]

One month later, nevertheless, Murphy discovered that the I.T.G.W.U. had infiltrated the parcel service of the company, and he dismissed a hundred men. A form was subsequently issued to the motor men and conductors to be signed and returned to inspectors. It read: 'Should a strike of any sort of the employees of the company be called for by Mr Larkin or the I.T.G.W.U., I promise to remain at my post and to be loyal to the company.' At the same time, he paid off men in the dispatch department of the *Independent* who had also joined the Transport Union. Larkin then placed pickets on the dispatch department of the *Independent* and its sister paper, the *Evening Herald*. Later, when some tramway men expressed grievances against their company at I.T.G.W.U. headquarters, the union put forward demands on their behalf, which Murphy declined to accept as he had made it clear that he did not recognise the I.T.G.W.U. as a legitimate union. Larkin rallied support at a large meeting at Beresford Place, where he told the crowd: 'Mr Murphy says there will be no strike. I tell Mr Murphy that he is a liar. Not only is there to be a strike on the trams . . . we are going to win this struggle no matter what happens.'[16]

On the following day, Tuesday 26 August, the first day of Dublin Horse Show week, the great social event of the year, Larkin carried out his threat. Shortly before 10 a.m., as the crowds were making their way to Ballsbridge for the show, some 200 motor men and conductors left their cars without warning. The cars driven by men who were not members of the union were held up, with the result that the entire street from College Green to the General Post Office was lined with trams. It was deliberately planned to cause maximum disruption in the transport system, while concealing the relatively small number of men involved. Murphy acted immediately. By noon the congestion was cleared, and he claimed that only 150 out of 750 tram men had answered the call from the union and that the trams were running and the strike broken. That night a mass meeting was held by Larkin at which he declared: 'We can smash the Tramway Company in a few days, if the same determination and spirit exists as was seen today.'[17] Feelings ran high, and there were instances of violent attacks on trams and tramway men. The trams continued to run, nevertheless, and the strike appeared to have failed, as Murphy had found it easy to get replacements for the strikers.

At this juncture the authorities blundered, arresting three prominent trades unionists, P. T. Daly, William O'Brien and Councillor Thomas Lawlor, on charges of sedition, and proscribing a labour demonstration planned for Sunday 31 August. This gave Larkin his opportunity. He charged the authorities with acting 'at the dictation of William Martin Murphy'[18]; and publicly burning the proclamation banning the Sunday meeting, he let it be known that the meeting would go ahead in Sackville Street (O'Connell Street) and that he would be present. He then found refuge from the police in Countess Markievicz's house.

As Sunday approached, the police were called to deal with a number of serious disturbances: at Ringsend, where the tramway company's power station was situated; in Brunswick Street, where an *Independent* van was attacked; and there were clashes in Beresford Place, Talbot Street, Marlborough Street, Earl Street, and at Burgh Quay and Eden Quay, where an overstretched police force lost restraint and two men were bludgeoned to death. In all, on Saturday 30 August about 200 civilians and 30 constables were reported to have been treated for injuries.[19]

Next day, as people strolled in the sunshine in Sackville Street, many of them waiting to see if Larkin would appear, a large force of police arrived. At about 1.30 p.m. an apparently elderly man opened the french windows of the Imperial Hotel, Murphy's own establishment, pulled off the wig he was wearing, shouted that he had kept his promise, and stepped back inside to await the police.

As the latter threw a cordon around the entrance, a section of the crowd charged the cordon three times. Eventually, perhaps fearing that Larkin might be rescued by the crowd, the police were given the order to charge. Another body of police charged from another direction. The crowd were caught beween the two lines of baton-wielding constables. Panic ensued, many were trampled underfoot, and men and women were beaten indiscriminately. The scene shocked bystanders, though the main newspapers defended the police, who were described as trying to curb the reign of ruffianism being forced on the city under the red flag of anarchy. The police attack, however, served to unite the workers more than ever behind Larkin.

To Murphy and the Chamber of Commerce, Larkin seemed to be all but defeated. At the quarterly meeting of the Chamber on 2 September 1913 Murphy commented that 'it was time to stop this man, and I think I have stopped him', and he added boldly, to applause, 'that some employers in Dublin had bred "Larkinism" by the neglect of their men and then they continued to support him by not having the courage to stand up against him'. Two days afterwards, however, Murphy and the city's major employers made their major blunder. Pressing home their advantage, they decided to shut out any of their employees who were members of the Irish Transport and General Workers' Union. Within days workers were asked to sign a document which required them 'to carry out all the instructions' given them by or on behalf of their employer, and obliged them 'to immediately resign' their 'membership of the Irish Transport and General Workers' Union (if a member) and . . . further undertake' that they would 'not join, or in any way support this union'.[20] Not to be a member was one thing, but to be obliged to forfeit one's right to join the union of one's choice was a very different matter. By 22 September the number of workers affected by the strike had risen to an approximate 20,000, and 14,000 of these depended on strike pay from the workers' central lock-out fund.

Both Murphy and Larkin had envisaged a short conflict. This was now no longer likely. British unions, seeing a central principle at stake, rallied to the support of the Dublin workers. The first of their food-ships arrived on 27 September. With the prospect of a long struggle and the concomitant loss of money for employers, there was a temptation to make concessions. Murphy settled himself to endure, and to stiffen the resolve of his fellow-employers. He became, even more than previously, the *bête noire* of Larkin's followers: 'It's all due to William Martin Murphy, William Martin Murphy.'[21] The hardship of the lock-out and the obduracy of the employers soon began to find other critics too, when the employers refused to meet British labour leaders in conference, proved unamenable to overtures from the Dublin Industrial Peace Committee, chaired by Professor Tom Kettle, and finally stood out against the recommendations of a special court of inquiry, which had been set up by the Board of Trade under the chairmanship of Sir George Askwith, a respected figure in industrial relations in England.

The hearings of the court of inquiry, which commenced on 29 September, were held in public and excited much interest, partly, indeed, because of the exchanges between Tim Healy, representing the employers, and Larkin, who himself represented the workers. Larkin seemed determined to discredit the statements made by employers, and as part of the process indulged in personal attacks and unsubstantiated allegations. On 3 October he faced Murphy in the witness-box. The latter insisted on standing, giving as his reason that his voice was weak. Larkin towered above him. A well-known literary figure in Dublin, John Eglinton (W. K. Magee), who was present on the occasion, recalled 'the dark inchoate face of Larkin and . . . his tall ungainly figure, craning forward as he bellowed forth his arraignment; and opposite him the calm handsome face of Murphy, with trim white beard, speaking just above his breath and glancing occasionally at his angry foe'.[22]

Murphy's cool and collected manner was briefly upset by an invidious question: 'Did you say that you would drive the late Mr Parnell to his grave or into the lunatic asylum?'

Murphy riposted sharply: 'I did not. That is an infamous lie.' And he availed of further probing from his interrogator to lay the vicious libel to rest.[23]

Thereafter Larkin seemed disconcerted at times by his opponent. 'You complain bitterly I have been attacking you in the columns of a paper called the *Irish Worker*?' he asked.

'I did not complain,' the witness replied quietly.

'You stated yesterday that I suggested that you should be murdered?' was the next question.

'I stated that what appeared in the paper was an incitement to murder,' answered the witness, and he added with emphasis, '—and so it was.'

Later on the question was put: 'Did you ever get a report that I or any official of the union went about your premises and interfered with any of your men?'

Murphy dryly replied: 'I have no report. With regard to yourself personally, you are generally in a safe place.' To which Larkin riposted:

'Yes, you generally see that I am put there (*laughter*).'[24]

'Did I ever make a statement that I didn't make good?' the cross-examiner continued.

'You said you would paralyse the trams, and you did not make it good,' responded his witness.

There was much more of this cut-and-thrust, without Larkin being able to ruffle again the calm, controlled demeanour of his antagonist.[25]

In his summing up, the labour leader depicted with passionate eloquence the deplorable social conditions prevailing in Dublin, which he laid at the doors of the employers; and he then went on to level against them, and especially Murphy, allegation after allegation. The leniency afforded Larkin to make charges unsupported by evidence, with no opportunity granted to the other side to rebut them, caused dissatisfaction among the Employers' Federation and moved Archbishop Walsh, who had little sympathy for Murphy and much for the workers, to wonder 'how any competent commissioner', let alone 'one known to be an able lawyer', 'could have conducted an inquiry in such an extraordinary fashion'.[26]

When the court of inquiry issued its report (the Askwith report) on 6 October 1913, the employers focused on those very points and on the inquiry's criticism of the use of sympathetic strikes, while endeavouring to play down its condemnation of employers as acting 'contrary to individual liberty' in obliging workers to sign the anti-union document. Finally, the employers declared that while it was in no way their province 'to interfere with the internal management of trades unions', they were 'compelled again to refuse to recognise the union' until, firstly, it was 'reorganised on proper lines' and, secondly, had 'new officials', who 'met with the approval of the British Joint Labour Board'. In the meantime they regretted that they would have to insist that workers continue to sign the undertaking against the union as it stood.[27]

The employers' stand provoked criticism from the newspapers not controlled by Murphy. They had by their attitude 'played into the hands of the agitator', declared *The Times*, 'and given substance to the charge that they care for nothing but money',[28] while the *Irish Times* modified its position of support for the employers and sought a quick solution. The *Freeman's Journal* went further, and printed an open letter to the 'Masters of Dublin' written by the much-respected AE, otherwise George W. Russell, editor of the *Irish Homestead*:

> You were within the rights society allows you when you locked out your men and insisted on the fixing of some principle to adjust your future relations with labour, when the policy of labour made it impossible for some of you to carry on your enterprises . . . But, having once decided on such a step, knowing how many thousands of men, women, and children, nearly one-third of the population of this city, would be affected, you should not have let one day to have passed without unremitting endeavours to find a solution of the problem. What did you do? . . . You determined deliberately in cold blood to starve out one-third of the population of this city, to break the manhood of the men by the sight of the suffering of their wives and the hunger of their children.

And with prophetic ring AE concluded:

> You may succeed in your policy [but] the men whose manhood you have broken will loath you . . . The children will be taught to curse you . . . The infant being moulded in the womb will have breathed into its starved body the vitality of hate . . . You are sounding the death-knell of autocracy in industry.[29]

Following the employers' rejection of the Askwith report, when the wave of sympathy was swelling in his favour, Larkin made two bad mistakes. He travelled to England to induce the significant unions there to support Dublin by means of sympathetic strikes, but the manner in which he did so antagonised many of those who supported him. Even more damaging was his decision to give approval to a scheme to alleviate the suffering of children affected by the lock-out by sending them to England. The plan, conceived in deep humanity, showed little understanding of the suspicions of proselytism to which it might give rise.

A storm of protest broke out in the newspapers. Indignant Catholics wrote to the archbishop. Priests complained. The Ancient Order of Hibernians interlinked politics and a religious zeal which evinced little concern for charity. Eventually Archbishop Walsh, who had sought to preserve a balanced stance between both sides, now felt obliged to speak out against what he regarded as ill-conceived actions which seemed to endanger the faith of his people. He attributed no false motives, as James Connolly fairly noted, but carried out the obligations which he judged to be required of him as a central pastor.

The plan for the 'deportation of children', as it was termed, attracted the attention of Catholics in Britain as well as in Ireland. There was much concern and planning in England, while in Ireland concern was linked to active, at times intemperate, opposition by clergy and laity to the actual departure of the children. The issue lost Larkin some supporters and many sympathisers and seemed to confirm the extravagant charges in the *Irish Catholic* and *Independent* newspapers that he was anti-religion, anticlerical, anarchic and a Marxist socialist.

The hysteria generated by the 'deportation scheme' helped stiffen the resistance of the employers, some of whom were finding it difficult to stand over 'the signatories' conditions' which the inquiry report had judged 'contrary to individual liberty'. Signs of this wavering had appeared on 27 November 1913 when a notice of motion was presented to the council of the Chamber of Commerce with a view to having it raised at the quarterly meeting on 1 December. It proposed that

> Whilst determinedly opposed to the principle of sympathetic strikes with their attendant disastrous effects to employers and workers, [we] are of the opinion that the employers in the interest of peace and goodwill ought to withdraw the agreement they have asked their workers to enter into in respect of the Irish Transport and General Workers' Union which the workers consider infringes their personal liberty.

The council, after debating the issue, announced formally that

> The council are unanimously of opinion that the discussion of these resolutions at the present time are [*sic*] undesirable, and the council decides not to bring such business before the quarterly meeting to be held on Monday, December 1st. The president is requested to announce the substance of the foregoing resolution to the meeting.[30]

It was the final closing of the ranks. British trade unions, for their part, refused to rally to Larkin's call for a general strike. Enthusiasm for his cause waned in face of his tumultuous militancy, and the trades union council was finding it increasingly difficult to sustain the weekly cash payment to the locked-out workers. Christmas, as a result, proved particularly cold and hungry. By mid-January 1914 the Transport Union found it impossible to prevent many workers drifting back to work on whatever terms they were offered.[31] By the end of January all was over.

III

At the annual meeting of the Dublin Chamber of Commerce on 28 January 1914 Murphy, the out-going president, 'was received with applause'. In his address he reviewed the events of the year at some length and then made reference to 'the labour disturbances which prevailed in Dublin during the last few months of the year'. He remarked:

> I was not conscious that I was opening a fresh chapter in the history of labour disputes when I took what appeared to be the only and natural course of defending by every means at my disposal a wanton attack on properties for which I was responsible.

'The strike', he continued, had been 'part of a plot to plunge the city into a state of anarchy and to make all business impossible' by means of 'a system known as "syndicalism" or "sympathetic strikes"' . . . Its avowed object was to destroy capitalists . . . and to establish what Mr Larkin called a "co-operative commonwealth" of which he, no doubt, was to be Cromwell.' 'There is, however, a fatal flaw in this scheme,' Murphy observed, 'as it makes no provision for maintaining the wage earned during the time that must elapse beween the destruction of the employer and the setting up of the "co-operative commonwealth" (*applause*).'

> It was strange enough [Murphy continued] that even the most ignorant labourer should be caught up by this claptrap, but it is amazing to think how the skilled tradesmen of the city, as represented by the Trades Council, came under the domination of Mr Larkin, and allowed themselves to be dragged at his tail (*applause*). The chief, if not the only cause of the slums of Dublin is the want of employment, especially for unskilled workmen. There are too many work people and too few employers. The remedy of the new social reformers for this sort of thing was, by withdrawing labour from them, to destroy the employers who, to save themselves, were forced to import new hands, and thus further glut the labour market. The method of improving the position of the workingmen seems to justify the derisive epithet of being an 'Irish way' of doing things.

But the Dublin Employers' Federation, Murphy affirmed, 'will not support any employer who does not agree to give his work people the full standard conditions of employment and wages current in his trade (*applause*)'. He then observed that what workers frequently failed to understand was 'that in ninety-nine cases out of a hundred they will get more out of their employers in anticipation of a strike than after it takes place. The threat of a strike has more terror for the employer than the strike itself'.[32]

In the aftermath of the strike, the Irish Transport and General Workers' Union was decimated and all but financially destroyed. Exhausted in body and mind, Larkin sought recuperation in what was supposed to be a short lecture tour in the United States of America. The sojourn, which commenced in October 1914, extended to eight and a half years. His long absence was to occasion deep divisions in the Transport Union and was to remove him, at a critical period in Irish history, from his position of virtually unchallenged leadership of the Irish labour movement. But the general or unskilled workers were the main victims of the bitter struggle. The more fortunate went back to work on condition that they severed their membership of the union. Hundreds of others were obliged to seek assisted passage to England and Scotland in search of work. By the end of

January 1915 the union's membership had fallen from an earlier estimated figure of 20,000 to some 3,500 paid-up members.[33]

Meanwhile the Chamber of Commerce took the unusual step of establishing a public committee to express formally their appreciation 'of the great services rendered by our ex-president, Mr William Martin Murphy, during the recent prolonged labour troubles'.[34] At the annual general meeting of the Chamber a year later, on 29 January 1915, it was reported that 'the response made in subscriptions' showed the citizens' appreciation of the services he had rendered to the city and the 'widespread feeling of esteem' for him. The testimonial would 'take the form of a portrait of Mr Murphy painted by the Irish artist, Mr William Orpen'. A replica, also by Orpen, would 'hang in the Chamber of Commerce'.[35] The presentation to Murphy of the portrait was made in February 1915, together with an inscribed address 'bearing the signatories of 410 noblemen and gentlemen representative of trade, commerce, and of the professions, not only in Dublin but throughout the country'. The address made particular reference to the strike period:

> When the recent labour troubles in Dublin arose, the stand taken by companies which you presided over, and your services on the Employers' Executive Committee, saved the city from a peril that threatened to destroy the industrial enterprises of the metropolis, as well as the rest of the country.

In his response, the normally restrained and modest Murphy allowed himself to bask for a while in the adulation of the business establishment, and even strayed briefly into the realms of rodomontade:

> There is one thing I will claim for myself, namely, that any part I have taken in the public life of Dublin has been free from self-seeking . . . To such public enterprises as I have been identified with in this city, I have given the strenuous exercise of all the faculties that I possess, and if my efforts have been in most cases crowned with success the result was mainly due to those who were associated with me. This was so in the case of the International Exhibition, and notably so in that of the Employers' Executive Committee, by whom the city was saved from the peril that threatend it . . . With regard

to the commercial undertakings with which my name is identified, they were, of course, embarked upon primarily with the object of making profit, [but the] making of profits has never been my leading idea in the various undertakings that I have projected. *To achieve something and to overcome obstacles in reaching my goal has always had a more stimulating effect on me than mere profit-seeking. To me . . . the game of business and the striving towards success in commerce is more fascinating than any form of sport* . . . I have carried the Irish flag far afield in commercial undertakings and I have proved that an Irishman, making his headquarters and spending his life in his native land, is not handicapped to such an extent as to prevent him from successfully extending his interests to Great Britain and abroad.[36]

A florid protestation, perhaps, but the sentiments indicate how strongly Murphy cherished his 'Irishness'. This, indeed, had been already clearly signalled in his attitude towards the Home Rule Bill for Ireland introduced in 1912.

6

HOME RULE, THE EASTER RISING AND PARTITION, 1912–17

I

The Irish Party's endorsement of the modest Home Rule Bill of 1912 hardened further Murphy's attitude to the party. The bill withheld authority from the proposed Irish Home Rule parliament not only in such areas as defence, peace or war, and the nature of relations with the crown, but even in the effective control of revenue, including the important area of customs and excise. This last, in Murphy's view, was a deprivation of something vital to a nation's identity, and consequently he and his *Independent* newspapers came out strongly against the measure. The Irish Party, for its part, continued, in Healy's words, its 'game of trying to make Murphy a sort of St Sebastian shot through with arrows', and especially in the area likely to hurt him most, his business enterprises. In 1913 Murphy's plans for the electrification of Kingstown (Dún Laoire), which had passed the committee stage in the House of Commons, were 'recommitted, contrary to the practice of parliament', thanks to the efforts of John Redmond.[1]

Meanwhile, a more formidable opposition to the Home Rule Bill had burst forth from northern Unionists led by Sir Edward Carson and vigorously supported by Andrew Bonar Law, leader of the British Conservative Party. This resulted in January 1913 in the formation of an Ulster Volunteer Force seeking Ulster's exclusion from the bill. This, in turn, begot a counter-force, the Irish Volunteers. The prospect of partition was being discussed as a serious, if temporary proposition; and the Irish Party, to Murphy's disgust, seemed likely to give way. Murphy was outraged, nevertheless, when on 9 March 1914 Prime Minister Asquith announced that each county in the province of Ulster and the county boroughs of Belfast and Derry were being permitted to decide by referendum whether they wished to be excluded from the Home Rule Act for a period of six years, and Redmond accepted the decision as 'the extreme limit of concession'. Murphy revealed to Healy that 'he had never lost a night's sleep during the tram strike; but was awake all night from humiliation after these pronouncements. He went into his office every night, for four nights afterwards (a thing he never did before), to keep the paper straight.'[2] The *Independent* condemned 'this mutilation of Ireland' as 'tantamount to permanent exclusion', and, despite protests from its editor, Murphy personally raised criticism of the party to a new pitch, dismissing its leaders as 'a place-hunting gang posing as patriots'.[3]

Such criticism, no doubt, weakened support for the party, but it did not mean that Murphy favoured insurrection to prevent the country being partitioned. Like most Irishmen of the day, he thought in terms of an adequate Home Rule settlement within the Empire and, indeed, was prepared to encourage recruitment to the British army following the outbreak of war in August 1914. His newspapers supported the war effort, and he personally appeared on a recruiting platform at the Mansion House, Dublin, on 5 September 1915 which he shared with John Redmond, Joseph Devlin, Lord Mayor Lorcan Sherlock and others, who were responding to Lord Kitchener's call the previous month for 10,000 men.[4] In the following November Murphy wrote to a conference of Dublin employers convened by the Lord Lieutenant, agreeing to facilitate enlistment 'by undertaking to keep men's positions open, and by some monetary encouragement as well'.[5] In addition, Murphy served as chairman of the Dublin Castle Red Cross Hospital. The Easter Rising took him, like most people, by surprise, and it was to lead not only to considerable material loss for him, but also, through the agency of the *Independent*, to one of the greatest embarrassments of his life.

From the opening of hostilities on Easter Monday until the *Irish Independent* reappeared on the streets on Tuesday morning eight days later, the country was without national newspapers and was alive with rumours. The *Independent*'s reappearance brought the first substantial news of the rising. Many people waited up half the night in Dublin until the first copies came off the press.

That issue, of 4 May, carried a ringing editorial, written by Harrington, presumably with Murphy's approval. Under the heading 'Criminal Madness', the editor declared that 'No term of

denunciation . . . would be too strong to apply to those responsible for the insane and criminal rising of last week. Around us, in
the centre of Ireland's capital, is a scene of ruin which is heart-
rending to behold.' These men, it was claimed, were 'the willing
dupes of Prussian intrigue'. Harrington made reference to Chief
Secretary Birrell's ineffective government, and to the incitement
to violence and irresponsibility by Carson, and issued a call for
leniency towards young men of under twenty-one years who were
innocently caught up in the insurrection. But 'the leaders who
organised and the prominently active spirits of the rising,
deserved', he declared, 'little consideration or compassion'. And
in the light of lives lost, and the enormous material damage, the
writer confessed that he cared little 'what is to become of the
leaders who are morally responsible for this terrible mischief'.

The carrying out of the death sentence on three of the
leaders, Patrick Pearse, Tom Clarke and Thomas MacDonagh, was
noted in the same issue. On the following day the executions were
recorded of Edward Daly, Michael O'Hanrahan, William Pearse
and Joseph Plunkett, only two of whom could be described as
'leaders'. On 6 May the paper recorded the death of Major John
MacBride. On 8 May it was the turn of Eamonn Ceannt, Michael
Mallin, and two nineteen-year-olds, Seán Heuston and Con
Colbert. The day-by-day account of executions gradually created a
change in public feeling and a surge of sympathy for the
executed and for the numerous prisoners. On 10 May the
Independent's editorial warned the government against a
backlash, stating that it 'must not be so severe as to create a
revulsion of feeling that would make martyrs of all or any of those
who have been sentenced'. It referred to Redmond's plea in the
House of Commons for clemency, and to Asquith's answer that
General Maxwell had been instructed to confine punishment to
narrower limits. At this point it seemed that there might be no
further executions, and that one of the main leaders—the
seriously wounded leader of the Irish Citizen Army, James
Connolly—would evade the maximum penalty. Connolly had
been an influential antagonist of Murphy during the 1913 labour
troubles.

Murphy, meanwhile, had been occupied in coping with
another result of the insurrection, namely the damage to

property. An indication of the damage was conveyed by Archbishop Walsh's secretary, Father Michael Curran, describing the sight which faced him in Sackville Street (O'Connell Street) just before the ceasefire, on the evening of Saturday 29 April 1916. 'There was not a soul but myself in the whole street,' he reported. 'The G.P.O. was a mere shell. The left-hand [i.e. east] side of Lower O'Connell Street was a smoking ruin. The right-hand side was little better. Clery's was burned out . . . The smell of burning materials pervaded everywhere. Smoke hung low about.'[6] Thus both of Murphy's premises, Clery's on one side of the street and the Imperial Hotel on the other, were destroyed.

Anxious to obtain recompense for damage sustained, and knowing the importance of moving quickly 'before public interest died away', Murphy organised a committee, composed largely of members of the Chamber of Commerce, to work with him. Following their preliminàry work, he called a major public meeting for 8 May. The Lord Mayor and Sir William Fry, also a member of the Chamber of Commerce, attended. The committee which Murphy had formed claimed damages, not just from the insurance companies, but also from the Local Government Board, for businesses damaged during the rising and for people thrown out of employment by reason of fires, and it aimed to have the names of these last forwarded to the Local Government Board, together with 'their salaries and conditions of employment, so that they might be assisted'. Sir William Fry expressed the thanks of the 'large representative meeting' to Murphy 'for his promptness in calling the meeting and the manner in which he had guided their deliberations', and a telegram was then sent to Prime Minister Asquith, signed by Murphy and other leading members of the Dublin Chamber of Commerce, requesting that he 'receive a deputation to lay their claims for compensation before the government at his earliest possible convenience'.[7] On foot of this, Murphy left for London to press their case.

While he was away Murphy's newspaper took a line which forever fixed him in working-class memory as a vindictive, unforgiving and cruel man. The *Irish Independent*, as well as warning the government against causing a revulsion of feeling, also advised it in an editorial: 'Let the worst of the ringleaders be singled out and dealt with as they deserve'; and the same issue carried a photograph of James Connolly with a caption: 'Still lies in Dublin Castle recovering from his wounds'. That was on 10 May. Two days later Connolly was executed. Even sixty years later it seemed to an eminent labour biographer that this was 'the crowning infamy' of Murphy's life; that having 'declared his policy', he 'crossed to London while the fuse burned'.[8] Yet the truth appears to have been otherwise.

'Without his knowledge or approval', Tim Healy observed, 'a leader was printed' by Murphy's newspaper 'which haunted him till his death'. And writing to his brother, Maurice, later in May 1916, Healy reported that Murphy told him that 'he did not know of the articles in the *Independent* recommending "vigour" until his attention was called to them afterwards'. 'He was greatly affected', Healy continued, 'by the thought that he had been accused of advising the shooting of Connolly, and said that, so far from it being true, he used to pray for Connolly owing to the antagonism he showed him.' As to the insurgents generally, Murphy 'admitted that at first he felt bitter' against them 'owing to the burning of Clery's and the Imperial Hotel', but then 'finding the Tories gloating over the executions and the imprisonments "every drop of Catholic blood in my veins surged up" and he began like others to pity them'.[9] Thus Murphy, it would appear, would not publicly exonerate himself at the expense of his newspaper staff, and this serves as a further caution against simplified portrayals of him as a person of 'inflexible equanimity'[10] and callous insensitivity.

Healy, indeed, unwittingly reflected the complexity of Murphy's personality in two other letters to his brother Maurice. On 15 June 1918 he reported concerning a speech he wrote for presentation at the American embassy in London, that 'William Murphy spoke to me twice very warmly in praise of my American address, which is a great thing for so cold a man.'[11] Yet in April 1913, following Murphy's serious illness, that allegedly 'cold' man evoked from him these words: 'To say that your illness affected me would be a poor saying . . . I daresay I shall often differ and disagree with you in the future. I hope we may both be spared for such clashes, but, had anything happened to you without my saying how much I like you and feel obliged to you, I should have carried a sorrow for what remains of life's skeleton to harbour. That you are restored is my abiding thanksgiving.'[12]

But to return to 1916. The Royal Commission on the Rebellion in Ireland sought Murphy's views on the insurrection. His comments, as usual, were forthright. Like many of his contemporaries, he laid much of the blame at the door of the Irish administration: 'That the authorities allowed a body of lawless and riotous men to be drilled and armed and to provide themselves with an arsenal of weapons and explosives was one of the most amazing things that could happen in any civilised country outside of Mexico.' That body of men, he pointed out, was allowed to hold meetings in uniform and 'discharge their rifles at night in the streets of Dublin without any attempt to check them or prosecute them'.[13]

In these words is reflected the frustration and anger of a great many constitutional nationalists, and they serve as a reminder that for every nationalist who bore arms at home, there were some sixteen Irishmen participating in a great war 'for the freedom of small nations'. Many of these also viewed their efforts as contributing to the gaining of Home Rule for their small nation. Murphy's nationalism was of a strong and vigorous nature, but it sought expression along constitutional lines: determined to achieve, within the political process, a form of Home Rule that included fiscal control and an integral, unpartitioned country. In quest of this goal, Murphy began to play a quietly influential role in the concluding months of 1916, and continued to do so in the two subsequent years.

II

In the aftermath of the 1916 insurrection, David Lloyd George, one of the most able of Asquith's cabinet, was entrusted with the unenviable task of working out an agreement between nationalists and unionists. He determined to interview a wide range of people. Rumours that he favoured partition were in the air, as were reports that a twenty-six-county Home Rule constitution would be enacted shortly. Murphy, in the *Irish Independent*, was 'slaughtering' the Irish Party, vociferous against partition, and pressing for a fuller form of Home Rule. On 8 June Lloyd George, who knew of Murphy through their mutual friend Alfred

Harmsworth, Lord Northcliffe, wrote requesting him 'not to make mischief in Ireland'.[14]

When on 12 June, however, the Ulster Unionist Council let it be known that they had accepted a 'definite' settlement, Murphy, while members of the Irish Party hesitated about the meaning of the announcement, correctly interpreted 'definite', and on 14 June wrote sarcastically to Lloyd George about the Ulster dove returning to the ark, 'having got all he ever asked for . . . a separate empire'.[15] He reminded Lloyd George that in his lifetime 'there were three rebellions in Ireland—in '48, '67, and 1916, all arising from the same cause, viz. the falling away of the independence of the Irish parliamentarians and their failure to assert themselves at Westminster'. He wanted 'the recent rebellion to be the last'.[16]

Murphy was aware that the Irish Party leadership were feeling so vulnerable in face of the rising tide of support for Sinn Féin that they were likely to sacrifice the nationalist majorities in Fermanagh, Tyrone and Derry city as a 'temporary arrangement'—so Lloyd George assured them—in return for immediate Home Rule.[17] Northcliffe invited him to London to discuss the partition negotiations and, after several interviews, insisted that he see Lloyd George. Murphy and Lloyd George appear to have had a number of meetings. In the course of them Murphy underscored his opposition to the partition scheme, warned that the exclusion of the Ulster counties would increase support for republican extremists both in the United States of America and in Ireland,[18] and in response to the question 'How would you settle the Irish question?', replied that he would do so in the same way as Britain settled the South African question, namely by Colonial Home Rule, and that it would not be settled in any other way. He added that as part of an Irish solution he would grant equal representation to Protestants and Catholics and would ensure that the former enjoyed a share of the executive power.[19]

Murphy's discussions with Lloyd George almost coincided with an attempt by the Solicitor-General, James O'Connor, to effect a united front between Murphy and Redmond and the Irish Party. The rapprochement did not get far. Murphy made it clear that while he had always regarded Redmond as 'an honourable gentleman', he disagreed with the policy and actions of his party and with Redmond's leadership. The latter's 'cardinal mistake as a leader', Murphy pronounced, had been that 'he failed to assert himself ' and 'allowed himself to fall under the dominion of others', at first O'Brien, Dillon and T. P. O'Connor, and later Joe Devlin, whose emphasis on place-seeking for party members led to the loss of party independence, and whose Ancient Order of Hibernians was a 'secret society of what Larkin aptly called Catholic Orangemen'. For the party to attach itself to the Liberal Party was a 'profound mistake', Murphy continued.[20] The members, in their anxiety to get power, blinded themselves to the imperfections of the Home Rule Act, leaving the power of taxation in the hands of an imperial parliament in which Irish representation was to be reduced by 63 members.

Murphy made it clear that much of his criticism of the Home Rule Act, and of the Irish Party's Home Rule policy, was greatly influenced by his reading of Erskine Childers's *Framework of Home Rule*, which he described as 'the best informed book that has ever been written on this subject'.[21] Childers had looked at the financial implications of Home Rule in terms of an examination of Home Rule in Canada and Australia, and particularly of the Home Rule Act of 1906 in South Africa; and he had emphasised the desirability of procuring this wider form of self-rule for Ireland. Hence Murphy's reference to South Africa in his conversations with Lloyd George.

'We really don't want, and never wanted any subsidy from England, if we were allowed to control our finances,' Murphy assured James O'Connor. ' Next year we shall be paying nearly three times what we were paying before the war—22 million against 8, or a 14 millions increase. We want the power to nurse or build up our own industries, which is denied under the Act in the statute book. We want, in fact, as near as circumstances will allow, Colonial Home Rule, and that would settle the question once for all.' The party as it then existed, Murphy added, was 'a source of weakness to Ireland, rather than strength'. When it was strong, it made no use of its power; and if there was currently the possibility of a larger measure of Home Rule, that was due 'not to the Party, but to the events of Easter Week'.[22]

The day after writing to O'Connor, Murphy sent to Lloyd George a set of carefully considered proposals. During the summer he had personally written a number of letters in the *Independent* criticising the Home Rule Act and pointing out that in order for it to be of 'material benefit to the Irish people' Home Rule would have to include 'control of customs and excise'.[23] Since then Lloyd George, assisted by Northcliffe's newspapers, had become Prime Minister, and Murphy hoped that in this position of power he might be induced to introduce measures more acceptable to the nationalist majority.

Murphy's proposals, briefly, were: to 'give Ireland the same fiscal and trade freedom as the colonies possess'; to 'provide for an equitable contribution from Ireland towards Imperial expenditure'; and to 'give the Protestant community half the representation in the National House of Commons'. And, as a further inducement to Unionists, Murphy suggested that they might be given a share of the local government of the country, from which they had been effectively shut out in twenty-six counties since the Local Government Act of 1898. Finally, as an enticement for the Prime Minister himself, who was greatly concerned at the appalling losses on the Western Front, Murphy added a fourth point under the heading of 'Manpower'. He suggested that 'in exchange for Colonial Home Rule, Ireland should accept compulsory service', though he doubted that 'naked conscription would be a practical scheme to put forward at once'. [24]

Murphy's suggestions appear to have had little or no effect, and in any event were most unlikely to receive support from the strong Conservative voice in the new coalition government. The entry of the United States of America into the war in April 1917, however, and the need to disarm Irish-American criticism of British rule in Ireland, pushed Lloyd George into signs of activity once more. He proposed yet again immediate Home Rule with six-county exclusion, or alternatively a convention of Irishmen who would themselves produce a scheme of self-government. The latter proposal had originated with Redmond and was widely welcomed. Lloyd George promised that the government would introduce immediate legislation to implement any 'substantial agreement' reached by the convention, but his main concern, as it turned out, was to shelve rather than solve Irish problems.[25]

7

CONVENTION AND CONSCRIPTION, 1917–18

I

On 16 May 1917 the Prime Minister outlined the terms of reference of the Irish Convention, in a letter to John Redmond, to the effect 'that Irishmen of all creeds and parties . . . meet together in a Convention for the purpose of drafting a constitution for their country which should secure a just balance of all the opposing interests . . .'. Invitations were extended to the chairmen of county councils, to six mayors, eight representatives of urban councils, to five nominees each from the Irish Parliamentary Party, the Ulster Unionist Council and the (southern) Irish Unionist Alliance. The Catholic hierarchy were invited to send four representatives, and the Archbishops of Dublin and Armagh were appointed to represent the Church of Ireland, and the Moderator of the General Assembly to represent the Presbyterian Church in Ireland. Invitations were extended also to the chairmen of the Chambers of Commerce of Dublin, Belfast and Cork, and to labour organisations, and to the representative peers of Ireland. Invitations intended to secure representation from the Sinn Féin party were declined, as were those extended to the Trades Councils of Dublin and Cork. Subsequently six persons were appointed to represent various labour organisations, and fifteen others were nominated by the government. In all, the membership came to ninety-five.[1]

The fact that Sinn Féin declined an invitation made it difficult to foresee a successful outcome. Expectations were further dimmed by a statement of Bonar Law that the Conservative Party would not be bound by the decision of the Convention;[2] and, of course, it was most unlikely that Ulster Unionists would reach agreement with the rest, since they had already secured their position as a result of the negotiations in 1914 and 1916. Nevertheless, there was some pressure on Unionists to co-operate because of the Empire's need for unity during the war, and the Chief Secretary in Ireland, H. E. Duke, was known to be opposed to partition, and had even persuaded Tim Healy that England too was against it.[3]

Duke invited Murphy to become a member of the Convention. His purpose in doing so, in Healy's view, was that the *Independent* might be less hostile.[4] After a considerable delay, Murphy, in the month of July, eventually accepted. The first meeting of the Convention took place shortly afterwards, on 25 July 1917 in the Regent House, Trinity College, Dublin, which, together with a number of offices, had been placed at the disposal of the gathering. Sir Horace Plunkett, an Irish Protestant, who was generally popular because of his work for the agricultural co-operative movement, was elected chairman, and Sir Francis Hopwood secretary. Erskine Childers was summoned to act as assistant. In keeping with Childers's adventurous life, the summons is reputed to have reached him by wireless while he was fighting in the air against the Germans.[5]

The first few meetings were devoted to establishing the general course of procedure to be followed. With such a large unwieldy body, it was decided to set up a working party, entitled the Grand Committee, consisting of twenty members. The Committee, which met twenty-two times, was composed of five Ulster Unionists, four southern Unionists, six Nationalists (including John Redmond and Patrick O'Donnell, Bishop of Raphoe), and three independent nationalists, namely Murphy, Edward Lysaght and George W. Russell (AE), who provided some link with Sinn Féin because of their independence of Redmond. Two labour representatives were also selected.[6]

It was decided that the Convention would commence with a 'presentation stage'. The various schemes for the future government of Ireland which had been communicated to the Convention would be considered first by the Grand Committee, and if deemed suitable for discussion would then be presented to the Convention. When these schemes were presented, there were to be no decisions made on them, and criticism and comment was to be directed towards improving the proposals. All this was to ensure full and frank discussion, and to enable members to know each other's point of view with a minimum of conflict. And in order to familiarise members with different parts of the country, meetings were to be held in Belfast and Cork, as well as in Dublin.

On 21 August 1917 Plunkett requested Murphy to introduce 'a Draft Bill for the self-government of Ireland on Dominion lines' and to invite proposals from others. The proceedings up to this 'had been educational', Murphy observed, but now they had to move towards solutions. After a preamble, partly in praise of Childers's *Framework of Home Rule*, Murphy declared that he had long ago come to the conclusion 'that the only road to the pacification of Ireland' was the one that proved successful in Canada and South Africa. And he quoted Sir Charles Gavan Duffy, the insurgent of 1848 and later Prime Minister of Victoria, who observed, with reference to the Irish question, that 'Canada did not get Home Rule because she was loyal and friendly, she is loyal and friendly because she got Home Rule'.[7]

The basic principle of his proposal, therefore, was 'that the Imperial parliament surrenders its power of legislating for Ireland and delegates to an Irish parliament full power to make laws for Ireland, with certain specific limitations'. In Murphy's scheme, these exceptions were 'the Crown, and Lord Lieutenant, peace and war, the navy and army, dignities and titles, treason, and naturalisation', but on no account would he make an exception of 'the Irish parliament's full and exclusive power to impose and collect taxes in Ireland, including custom duties, and to apply their proceeds and all other Irish revenues to the public service of Ireland'. Those words of Childers, he proclaimed, were of 'the essence of self-government'.[8] He went on to assure Unionists of fair treatment under an 'Irish colonial government', and contrasted that situation with what could prevail under a nine-county Ulster legislature where, he declared, there would be a majority of Catholics legislating for Protestants in the sensitive area of education, while if Ulster were only six counties, there would be a majority of Protestants legislating for Catholics. 'A parliament for all Ireland would be much more likely to do justice for both.'[9]

Throughout the deliberations Murphy emphasised fiscal autonomy, and the addresses he presented on the control of customs and excise were acknowledged as models of lucidity.[10] His mastery of matters fiscal caused disarray at times in nationalist ranks. Thus on 6 November 1917, in response to queries from

Irish Party representatives on the implications of the Home Rule Act for Irish industries, he pointed out that past experience had shown that no regard was had for Irish interests which did not harmonise with British interests, and hence under the projected fiscal union 'Ireland would be unable to encourage new industries or protect industries from "dumping"'. His competence and influence resulted in his being appointed to a special sub-committee of nine set up to find a basis for agreement from the many schemes submitted to the Convention. He took his work in the Convention so seriously that 'he put aside all other interests to concentrate on it',[11] and his newspapers promoted his views on the matters discussed by the Convention.

The combination of Murphy's sharp mind and influential journals proved too much for an ailing John Redmond. Already on 30 September 1917, when Plunkett tried to persuade the party leader to draw up a scheme to be the basis for discussion in the Grand Committee, he declined for fear of 'falling foul of W. M. Murphy'. He advised that Bishop O'Donnell be asked instead.[12] Subsequently Murphy was exultant when the strength of his case for fiscal freedom led O'Donnell and Joe Devlin to desert Redmond and support his demand. 'Anchored on realities,' Healy remarked graphically, 'he rejected peaches painted on canvas' and 'could not be flustered or drawn from his purpose'. He 'was strong against Redmond's jelly-fishness, and said he was continuously giving away one thing after another, until in the end nothing was left'.[13]

For all Murphy's efforts, however, there was not a united report. 'Although the Convention, with the exception of the Ulster delegates, nearly came to agreement,' the supportive Lord Dunraven commented, 'it fizzled out in confusion'.[14] In the end Murphy, together with twenty-one others—including Archbishop John Harty of Cashel, Bishops Patrick O'Donnell of Raphoe and Joseph MacRory of Down and Connor, and Joe Devlin—produced and signed a minority report.[15]

In April 1918 Plunkett presented the majority report at Downing Street. It could not claim to represent the 'substantial agreement' sought, and Lloyd George was not in a very receptive frame of mind. In the previous month the Germans had broken the military deadlock, which had prevailed since the start of the

war, by crashing through the Allied lines in France. The need for
fresh troops to throw into the front was critical. The obvious
source was Ireland. The other members of the United Kingdom
had been experiencing compulsory conscription since 1916. The
Easter Rising had deferred decision regarding Ireland. The
British Prime Minister appears to have hoped that 'substantial
agreement' at the Convention would enable him to introduce
Home Rule, and link with it the application of conscription.[16]

In the event, Horace Plunkett handed in his report on the
morning of 10 April, and that afternoon, attending the House of
Commons, was taken aback to hear Lloyd George introduce a
Military Service Bill which gave the government power to apply
conscription by order in council when the need arose. He
coupled it with a pledge to introduce a Home Rule measure
before the conscription provision came into effect; but by this
time few trusted British promises, and the attention of all, apart
from Unionists in the north-east of Ireland, focused on conscription. The Convention was past history.[17]

II

Chief Secretary Duke had warned the cabinet that the
measure on conscription would unite all Catholics and nationalists against the government. He proved correct. Some 200,000
Irishmen had already gone to fight in the war. Those at home had
no wish to be obliged by an English parliament to face death in
'England's war'. Public indignation was such that when the bill
was passed the Irish Party withdrew from Westminster. Sinn Féin,
the Irish Party, Labour and various independent groups,
supported by the Irish Cathoic bishops, joined together in opposition. An anti-conscription pledge was drawn up by de Valera and
taken by all shades of nationalists. Labour called a one-day strike
which operated with wide-ranging effectiveness. Anti-British
feeling was intense; and determination to resist conscription to
the end was increasingly expressed. The government added to the
resentment by appointing to the position of Lord Lieutenant a
field-marshal, Lord French. Shortly after his arrival in May 1918

the chief leaders of Sinn Féin were arrested. Not imprisoned, however, was Michael Collins, whose organisational genius now found full scope as he built up an intelligence service in the police force, the Post Office and elsewhere and worked with other key figures in retraining the Volunteers and preparing them for violent confrontation.

A feature of the opposition to conscription was the vigour and intensity of the campaign waged by the *Independent* newspapers and the ancillary *Irish Catholic*. Murphy had become, as Healy observed in September 1918, 'astonishingly nationalist in an active way'.[18] In the end the government backed down in face of outraged, highly orchestrated resistance. The war came to a close in November 1918 without conscription being imposed in Ireland. The threat, however, and their powerful response to it, gave new impetus to Sinn Féin and the cause of nationalism; and, in the general election at the end of the year Sinn Féin, despite government harassment, achieved an overwhelming success, and the Irish Party all but disappeared.

In January 1919 the elected members of Sinn Féin invited all elected representatives to an Assembly of Ireland, or the first Dáil Éireann, at the Mansion House, Dublin. Only the Sinn Féin members attended. They ratified the establishment of the Irish Republic proclaimed in 1916, and pledged themselves and their people to make this declaration of independence effective by every means at their command. It was a young assembly. Nearly three-quarters of the members were under forty-five, and only ten per cent had any experience of local government. Almost all were Catholics.[19] It was a new political world within a short space of time.

How Murphy viewed the bewildering rate of change is not too clear. One side of him, undoubtedly, welcomed the collapse of the Irish Party, but this could scarcely resign him to the growing republicanism and violence associated with Sinn Féin. He had wanted a strong, independent Home Rule Ireland, which preserved the link with the monarchy and the Empire, and, as a result, was presumably unhappy with the strident republicanism of the new Dáil and the political inexperience of so many of its members. But one could never be absolutely sure where William Martin Murphy was concerned.

As has been seen, Murphy had a youthful quality which gave him a remarkable facility for adapting to situations and new opportunities; after all, he was sixty years of age when he launched the new-look *Irish Independent*, and sixty-eight when he master-minded the employers' campaign of 1913 and kept it going relentlessly to the end. And had he lived, it seems likely that the imposition of martial law later in 1919, together with the virtual abolition of freedom of the press, of the right to public meeting, the right of personal liberty, even the right of trial by jury, in the final months of the year,[20] would have brought about once again a surge of nationalist blood in his veins and a deep resentment at being bullied. In the event, he never experienced those harsh realites. In June 1919 he was suddenly taken ill with a heart complaint at his residence, Dartry Hall, Upper Rathmines. At first his condition did not seem serious, but after a week, on the morning of the 26 June, he took a sudden turn for the worse, and he died later that day.[21] He was seventy-four years of age.

CONCLUSION

Following William Martin Murphy's death, national newspapers, numerous local journals and some periodicals wrote of his career. There was little or nothing about philistinism or about his starving many Dublin working-class families into submission; instead there was much about his business acumen and financial skills, his patriotic investment of his money in Ireland rather than abroad, and his belief in the country's possibilities and reserves. There was much too about his strength of character, which could refuse a Lord Lieutenant, inconvenience a king, and stand firm before intense public pressure; much about his courage, as he walked the streets of Dublin unescorted during the tense days of strike and lock-out; and much about his many works of charity.

Finally, there were references to the informal and leisure activities which have not figured in these pages: how he was the first captain of Milltown Golf Club, was president of the Rathgar and Rathmines Musical Society, and was an intrepid yachtsman from his early years, and a member of the Royal Irish and Royal Alfred Yacht Clubs at Kingstown (Dún Laoire), where he both cruised and raced with his twenty-five-foot yacht *Eva*. It was noted that he relaxed each year in his native Castletownbere and Bantry, where he was always Willie Murphy and felt among his own, for—as much as his antagonist James Larkin, though a generation earlier and in a rural setting—he too was conscious of being one of the 'risen people'. Beneath his boardroom eminence, striking personality and patrician manner, Murphy continued to view himself as he had done in 1895 when he told the electors that 'he belonged to the people' and that 'he felt himself belonging to the common clay of Ireland. It was in his nature and bones and he felt he could not put it out of them.'[1]

The comments in the British press were equally positive, though the *Daily Chronicle*, in its 'Office Window' column, focused on something different, yet distinctive, in an effort to understand his elusive personality. Having mentioned that when one met him one 'got the impression of an ascetic, kindly man of the diplomatic class, exceedingly well dressed, quiet spoken with a humorous twinkle in his eye, and no trace of a Dublin accent', the columnist added that 'His was a case of the iron hand in the velvet glove. Behind the blue eyes dwelt a soul of iron.' And he observed, seeking firmer delineation, that though Murphy was 'a native of Cork, his characteristics were more Scottish than Irish'.[2] By this, presumably, he had in mind, as well as Murphy's engineering and financial abilities, his hard-headed detachment—which to some seemed 'coldness'. Murphy himself, in fact, drew attention to this aspect in a letter to James O'Connor in December 1916, when he assured the Solicitor-General that he had no personal animus against John Redmond, and that he, Murphy, was singular as an Irishman in 'not allowing political disagreements to affect' his 'opinion of persons'.[3]

Such positive views, and efforts to understand, were swept aside in the new Ireland which took James Connolly and the 'martyrs' of 1916 into the pantheon of national heroes, and viewed a supposedly uncultured bourgeois businessman, who was also seen as the capitalist tyrant of 1913, as even more reprehensible than John Redmond and other members of the Irish Party, who were dismissed as not being 'Irishmen'.[4] Generations later, however, and in a wider European context, when economic development and employment occupy centre stage, and Yeats's image of the businessman as a lesser being, fumbling in the greasy till, has given way to a positive conception of business and its contribution to national well-being, in this setting there is an openness, perhaps, to a renewed appreciation of Murphy, as there already is of Redmond.

At his death Murphy left a personal estate of over a quarter of a million pounds. He also left to posterity his highly organised tramway system, which was subsequently and short-sightedly destroyed, and which appears likely to be reintroduced in some form in years to come. He also left his *Independent* newspapers. The latter pursued a policy of which he would probably have approved, in supporting the Treaty of 1921 and the Irish Free State. He would undoubtedly have experienced considerable satisfaction at the buying out in 1924 of the *Freeman's Journal* by the *Independent*.

Not the least of Murphy's many achievements was the fact that his newpapers had helped in the spread of literacy, while at the same time forwarding an early information revolution, moulding political opinion, and providing many hours of entertainment. All in all, to paraphrase the judgement in recent years of Professor Donal McCartney, 'it would be difficult to exaggerate' the impact this lone 'press baron' has had on Irish life.[5]

NOTES

1

[1] Address of Dr Lombard Murphy to staff of Independent Newspapers Ltd, 29 June 1941, on the occasion of their presentation to him to mark the completion of twenty-one years as chairman of the company (Murphy Papers, in keeping of Gerald Murphy, Dublin, great-grandson of William Martin Murphy).

[2] *The Belvederian*, 1909, p. 34.

[3] Ibid., pp 35–6

[4] Ibid., 1920, p. 25.

[5] Ibid., 1909, p. 38.

[6] Family Notes and genealogical tree compiled by Lombard Murphy for private circulation (Murphy Papers).

[7] Lombard Murphy, Address, p. 13.

2

[1] *Irish Independent*, 29 June 1919.

[2] T. P. O'Connor, *Memoirs of an Old Parliamentarian* (2 vols, London, 1929), ii, p. 58.

[3] Lombard Murphy, Address, pp 13–14.

[4] Mary E Daly, *Dublin: The Deposed Capital* (Cork, 1984), pp 172–3.

[5] *Dublin United Tramway Co. Ltd. Meeting of Motormen, Conductors etc. held in the Antient Concert Rooms at the invitation of the Chairman, soon after Midnight of Saturday, 19 July, 1913* (NLI, LO P83).

[6] Arnold Wright, *Disturbed Dublin: The Story of the Great Strike of 1913–14* (London, 1914), pp 69–70.

[7] Ibid., p. 70.

[8] Railway Records Library and Archives (Heuston Station, Dublin).

[9] Dublin Diocesan Archives (DDA), McCabe Papers, Laity file, 1882: proxy paper signed by Cardinal McCabe.

[10] O'Connor, *Memoirs*, ii, 54

[11] Regulation of Railways Act, 1868, and subsequent definitions, in J. C. Conroy, *A History of Railways in Ireland* (London, 1928), pp 236–8.

[12] For Murphy's links with the different lines see Irish Railway Reports, half-yearly, from 1885 to 1912 (Railway Records Library and Archives).

[13] Ibid., pp 89–90.

[14] Ibid., p. 119.

[15] Alexander Sullivan, *Old Ireland*, quoted in Lombard Murphy, Address, p. 27.

[16] W. M. Murphy, *The Irish Industrial Question* (address to Wood Quay National Registration Club, 10 Jan. 1887) (Trinity College, Dublin (TCD), 191. c. 22, no. 8), p. 10.

[17] Ibid., p. 12.

[18] Ibid., pp 23–4.

[19] T. M. Healy, *Letters and Leaders of My Day* (2 vols, London, 1928), i, 243.

[20] Ibid., p. 307. Healy recounts how Murphy obliged Parnell at an auction by purchasing a weighing-machine for him and then, with care, forwarded it to his Wicklow home, but never received even the courtesy of an acknowledgement, let alone recompense. Murphy, as Healy remarked, was too proud to dun him for it.

[21] O'Connor, *Memoirs,* ii, 56.

[22] Ibid., p. 58.

3

[1] See Emmet Larkin, *The Roman Catholic Church in Ireland and the Fall of Parnell, 1888–1891* (Chapel Hill, 1979), pp 218–20.

[2] Ibid.

[3] DDA, Walsh Papers, Laity file, 1890, 404/4–6: Murphy to Walsh, Nov. 1890 (no other date).

[4] Ibid.: Walsh to Murphy, 30 Nov. 1890.

[5] Ibid.: Murphy to Walsh, 30 Nov. 1890.

[6] Ibid.

[7] *Freeman's Journal,* 1 Dec. 1890, quoted in Larkin, *Roman Catholic Church,* p. 223, and by P. J. Walsh, *William J. Walsh, Archbishop of Dublin* (Dublin, 1928), p. 416.

[8] Walsh, *Walsh,* p. 418.

[9] DDA, Walsh Papers, Laity file: Walsh to Murphy, 5 Dec. 1890.

[10] Ibid. Murphy to Walsh, 6 Dec. 1890.

[11] Ibid.

[12] Ibid.

[13] F. S. L. Lyons. *Charles Stewart Parnell* (London, 1978 ed.), p. 536.

[14] DDA, Laity file: Murphy to Walsh, 12 Dec. 1890.

[15] Ibid.: Murphy to Walsh, 17 Dec. 1890.

[16] Ibid.: Murphy to Walsh, Dec. 1890 (no other date).

[17] Larkin, *Roman Catholic Church,* pp 253–4.

[18] DDA, Laity file: Murphy to Walsh, 23 Dec. 1890.

[19] Ibid., Prelates file: Manning to Walsh, Christmas 1890.

[20] Larkin, *Roman Catholic Church,* p. 254.

[21] Healy, *Letters and Leaders,* i, 355–6.

[22] Ibid., ii, 361.

[23] Larkin, *Roman Catholic Church,* p. 263.

[24] DDA, Laity file: Murphy to Walsh, 9 Apr. 1892.

[25] Ibid.: Murphy to Walsh, 14 Jan. 1893.

[26] Ibid.: Walsh to Sexton, 10 Jan. 1893.

[27] Ibid.: Dillon to Walsh, 17 Jan. 1893.

[28] Ibid.: Walsh to Sexton, 7 Mar. 1893 (draft).

[29] Ibid.: Dillon to Walsh, undated, but in file for 1893.

[30] F. S. L. Lyons, *John Dillon* (London, 1968), pp 168–9; see also Healy, *Letters and Leaders,* ii, 423.

[31] Lyons, *Dillon,* pp 170–71.

[32] *'Liffey at Ebb Tide', Mr T. M. Healy, M.P., on Mr Wm O'Brien, M.P., and vice versa* (pamphlet produced by United Irish League, 1910, to discredit Healy and O'Brien, who had recently united against the Irish Party), p. 35.

[33] Redmond to Healy, 31 July 1900, quoted in Healy, *Letters and Leaders,* ii, 449.

[34] T. M. Healy to his brother Maurice, 3 Aug. 1900, in proofs of Healy, *Letters and Leaders*, quoted in Frank Callanan, *T. M. Healy* (Cork, 1996), p. 439.

[35] *Irish Independent*, 27 June 1919. The editor of the *Irish Catholic* since 1888 had been W. F. Dennehy, and in 1912 Murphy transferred the copyright to him.

[36] DDA, Walsh Papers, Laity file, July 1901.

[37] NLI, Redmond Papers, MS 15209: Murphy to Redmond, 27 Sept. 1900.

[38] Ibid.: Murphy to James O'Connor, K.C., 11 Dec. 1916.

[39] Callanan, *Healy*, p. 474.

[40] *Handbook to the Dublin District* (1908), produced by British Association, London, p. 397.

[41] O'Connor, *Memoirs*, ii , 55–6.

[42] Ibid., p. 57.

4

[1] *Irish Independent*, 27 June 1919.

[2] Arnold Wright, *Disturbed Dublin: The Story of the Great Strike of 1913–14* (London, 1914), pp 69–71.

[3] Callanan, *Healy*, p. 711 n. 31

[4] Hugh Oram, *The Newspaper Book: A History of Newspapers in Ireland, 1649–1983* (Dublin, 1983), p. 106.

[5] Lombard Murphy, Address, p. 21.

[6] Gerard Harrington, 'A Loyal Son of Beara' (published article, with no title of paper or magazine, in Murphy Papers); see also Oram, *Newspaper Book*, p. 103.

[7] Oram, *Newspaper Book*, p. 103.

[8] *Irish Independent*, Golden Jubilee edition, 3 Jan. 1955.

[9] *Irish Independent*, 2 Jan. 1905, quoted in Lombard Murphy, Address, p. 23.

[10] *Irish Independent*, 27 June 1919.

[11] Oram, *Newspaper Book*, pp 108–9.

[12] Healy to Maurice Healy, 27 Nov. 1915, 17 Aug. 1918, quoted in Callanan, *Healy*, p. 484.

[13] O'Connor, *Memoirs*, ii, 57–8.

[14] Murphy to Harrington, 23 Oct. 1910, quoted in Callanan, *Healy*, p. 484.

[15] Healy to Maurice Healy, 5 Jan., 14 Feb. 1914, 22 May 1916, quoted ibid., pp 485–6.

[16] Donal McCartney, 'William Martin Murphy, Press Baron' (Thomas Davis Lecture, 30 Oct. 1983); notes by Gerald Murphy (Murphy Papers).

[17] Quoted in Callanan, *Healy*, pp 485–6.

[18] Summary notes by Gerald Murphy (Murphy Papers), p. 39.

[19] Healy to Maurice Healy, 13 Mar. 1917, quoted in Callanan, *Healy*, p. 530.

[20] D.C.C., 'Report of the Council for 1919 at Annual General Meeting, 30 Jan. 1920', pp 8–9 (NLI, I.380.941.D.4).

[21] Wright, *Disturbed Dublin*, p. 77.

[22] Ibid.

[23] D.C.C., Report of Council, 30 Jan. 1920 (NLI, I.380.941.D.4).

[24] D.C.C., 'Report for 1911' (ibid.), pp 11–12.

[25] D.C.C., 'Report for 1912' (ibid.), pp 34–8.

[26] R. P. Davis, *Arthur Griffith and Non-Violent Sinn Féin* (Dublin, 1974), p. 13.

[27] F. S. L. Lyons, *Culture and Anarchy in Ireland* (Oxford, 1982), pp 75–6.

[28] *Irish Independent,* 22 Jan. 1913, quoted in Callanan, *Healy,* pp 486–7.

[29] For the Chamber of Commerce debate see Report of Council to Members of D.C.C., 12 Aug. 1913 (National Archives (NAI), 1064/2/1–2).

[30] Lyons, *Culture and Anarchy,* p. 76.

[31] Conor Cruise O'Brien, *Passion and Cunning and Other Essays* (London, 1988), pp 23–4. O'Brien observes that it was only after Archbishop Walsh intervened against the 'deportation' of the children that Yeats suddenly took an interest and wrote to the *Irish Worker* in criticism of employers, clergy, press and police.

[32] Healy to Maurice Healy, 19 Nov. 1900, quoted in Healy, *Letters and Leaders,* ii, 453, and in Callanan, *Healy,* p. 708 n. 66.

5

[1] J. W. Boyle, *The Irish Labour Movement in the Nineteenth Century* (Washington, 1988), pp 250–51, 115–16.

[2] Arthur Griffith in *Sinn Féin,* 28 Nov. 1908, quoted in Dermot Keogh, *The Rise of the Irish Working Class* (Belfast, 1982), p. 129.

[3] James Connolly, *The Axe to the Root* (1908), quoted in Keogh, *Rise of the Irish Working Class,* p. 158. Connolly's syndicalism envisaged one great union with vertically organised syndicates, or departments, of industry; the representatives elected from these various syndicates would meet 'and form the industrial administration or national government of the country'.

[4] NLI, O'Brien Papers, MS 13908 (2): Connolly to William O'Brien, 23 July 1913.

[5] The prospect of a prolonged rail strike, and its impact on the British navy's coal supplies, proved too much for the government at a time when the assertion of German naval strength at Agadir, off Morocco, was raising the spectre of war with Germany.

[6] D.C.C. Council Minutes, 21 Sept. 1911 (NAI, 1064/3/16).

[7] D.C.C., Report of Council to General Meeting, 27 Sept. 1911, pp 354–5 (NAI, 1064/2 /1–2).

[8] Transcript of G.S.W.R. Company minutes, 27 Sept. 1911, in Peter Rigney, 'Trade Unionism and the Great Southern and Western Railway, 1890–1911' (B.A. thesis, Trinity College, Dublin), p. 53.

[9] Ibid., p. 63. Much of the account of the strike comes from this source.

[10] D.C.C. Council Minutes, 27 Sept. 1911 (NAI, 1064/3/16).

[11] D.C.C., Report of Council to General Meeting, 2 Nov. 1911, pp 359–61 (NAI, 1064/2/1–2). The resolution was defeated by 30 votes to 23 votes.

[12] D.C.C., Report of Quarterly Meeting, 2 Sept. 1913, p. 398 (ibid.).

[13] Ibid.; see also D.C.C., Report of Annual Meeting, 28 Jan. 1914, p. 403 (ibid.). As regards Murphy's illness, he was missing from the meetings of 10 March and 14 April, and the Council Minutes of 5 May 1913 record Mr Pim announcing the pleasure of all 'to see the president back again after his severe illness' (NAI, 1064/3/16).

[14] *Irish Worker,* 7 Sept. 1912.

[15] '*Dublin United Tramway Co. Ltd. Meeting of Motormen, Conductors etc. held in the Antient Concert Rooms at the invitation of the Chairman, soon after Midnight of Saturday, 19 July, 1913'* (NLI, LO P83).

[16] *Daily Express,* 26 Aug. 1913.

[17] *Freeman's Journal,* 27 Aug. 1913.

[18] *Daily Express,* 30 Aug. 1913.

[19] *Evening Telegraph,* 31 Aug. 1913; see Keogh, *Rise of the Irish Working Class,* p. 199.

[20] *Freeman's Journal,* 5 Sept. 1913.

[21] DDA, Priests file: Father Michael Curran to Walsh, 12 Sept. 1913.

[22] John Eglinton, *A Memoir of AE—George William Russell* (London, 1937), p. 86.

[23] Quoted in Emmet Larkin, *James Larkin, Irish Labour Leader, 1876–1947* (London, 1989 ed.), p. 133; see also Callanan, *Healy,* p. 488.

[24] *Freeman's Journal,* 4 Oct. 1913.

[25] Wright. *Disturbed Dublin,* pp 198–9.

[26] DDA, Laity file: Walsh to Lord Aberdeen, 10 Oct. 1913.

[27] *Court of Enquiry into Disputes in Dublin. Employers' Reply to Sir George Askwith's Findings* (printed document in DDA, Walsh Papers, Laity file, 14 Oct. 1913).

[28] Quoted in Keogh, *Rise of the Irish Working Class,* p. 217.

[29] Quoted in *1913: Jim Larkin and the Dublin Lockout* (Workers' Union of Ireland, Dublin, 1964), p. 57.

[30] D.C.C. Council Minutes, 27 Nov. 1913 (NAI, 1064/3/16).

[31] Thomas Morrissey, *A Man Called Hughes: The Life and Times of Séamus Hughes, 1881–1943* (Dublin, 1991), p. 43.

[32] D.C.C., Report of Annual Meeting, 28 Jan. 1914, p. 404 (NAI, 1064/2/1–2); see also *Irish Catholic,* 28 Jan. 1914.

[33] Morrissey, *A Man Called Hughes,* p. 47.

[34] D.C.C. Council Minutes, 9 Feb. 1914 (NAI, 1064/3/16).

[35] D.C.C., Report of Council for 1914 at Annual General Meeting, 29 Jan. 1915, pp 9–10 (NAI, 1064/1/9–17).

[36] *Irish Independent,* 27 June 1919 (my italics).

6

[1] Healy, *Letters and Leaders,* ii, 527–8.

[2] Healy to William O'Brien, 17 Mar. 1914, quoted in Callanan, *Healy,* p. 503.

[3] Notes by Gerald Murphy, p. 39 (Murphy Papers); see also Healy to O'Brien, 10, 17 Mar. 1914, quoted in Callanan, *Healy,* p. 502.

[4] J. V. O'Brien, *'Dear Dirty Dublin': A City in Distress, 1899–1916* (Berkeley, Calif., 1982), p. 252.

[5] *Irish Independent,* 24 Nov.1915, quoted in Callanan, *Healy,* p. 510.

[6] Reminiscences of Father Michael Curran (NLI, Seán T. Ó Ceallaigh Papers, Special List, A 9, MS 27728 (1), p. 68).

[7] *Irish Independent,* 9 May 1916.

[8] C. D. Greaves, *The Life and Times of James Connolly* (London, 1976), p. 420.

[9] Healy, *Letters and Leaders,* ii, 562.

[10] O'Connor, *Memoirs,* ii, 56.

[11] Healy, *Letters and Leaders,* ii, 601.

[12] Lombard Murphy, Address, 29 June 1941, p. 29 (Murphy Papers).

[13] *Royal Commission on the Rebellion in Ireland, Minutes of Evidence and Appendix of Documents* (London, 1916), pp 110–11, quoted in Arthur Mitchell and Pádraig Ó Snodaigh (eds), *Irish Political Documents, 1916–1949* (Dublin, 1985), p. 27.

[14] Lloyd George to Murphy, 8 June 1916, quoted in George Dangerfield, *The Damnable Question: A Study in Anglo-Irish Relations* (London, 1977), p. 231.

[15] Murphy to Lloyd George, 14 June 1916, quoted ibid., pp 321–2.

[16] Murphy to Lloyd George, June 1916, quoted in Callanan, *Healy,* p. 521.

[17] Michael Laffan, *The Partition of Ireland, 1911–1925* (Dundalk, 1983), pp 50–53.

[18] McCartney, 'William Martin Murphy, Press Baron'.

[19] NLI, Redmond Papers, MS 15209 (2): Murphy to James O' Connor, 20 Dec. 1916.

[20] Ibid.: Murphy to O'Connor, 11 Dec. 1916.

[21] Ibid.: Murphy to O'Connor, 20 Dec. 1916.

[22] Ibid.

[23] *Irish Independent*, 27 June 1919.

[24] NLI, Redmond Papers, MS 15209 (2): Murphy to Lloyd George, 21 Dec. 1916.

[25] Laffan, *Partition of Ireland*, p. 56.

7

[1] *Report of the Proceedings of the Irish Convention, 1918* (HMSO Dublin/London, 1918), p. 9.

[2] Healy, *Leteers and Leaders*, ii, 582.

[3] Healy to Maurice Healy, 2 June 1917, quoted ibid.

[4] Ibid., p. 585.

[5] Ibid., p. 583.

[6] D. W. Miller, *Church, State, and Nation in Ireland, 1898–1921* (Dublin, 1973), p. 366.

[7] *Irish Convention, 1917–1918. Speeches and Draft of a Home Rule Bill, by Wm M. Murphy*, p. 24 (NLI, Ir. 941, p. 241).

[8] Ibid.

[9] Ibid.

[10] *Irish Independent*, 27 June 1919.

[11] Ibid.

[12] Miller, *Church, State and Nation*, p. 366.

[13] Healy to Maurice Healy, 16 Jan. 1918, quoted in Healy *Letters and Leaders*, ii, 589; see also Callanan, *Healy*, p. 532.

[14] Lord Dunraven, *Past Times and Pastimes* (2 vols, London, 1922), ii, 60.

[15] *Report of Proceedings of the Irish Convention*, p. 43.

[16] David Lloyd George, *War Memoirs* (2 vols, London, 1938 ed.), ii, 1599.

[17] Trevor West, *Horace Plunkett: Co-operation and Politics* (Washington, 1986), p. 175.

[18] Healy to Maurice Healy, 6 Sept. 1918, quoted in Callanan, *Healy*, p. 532.

[19] F. S. L. Lyons, *Ireland since the Famine* (London, 1971), pp 400–5.

[20] *Freeman's Journal*, 10 Nov. 1919.

[21] *Irish Independent*, 27 June 1919.

Conclusion

[1] *Freeman's Journal*, 23 May 1895 quoted in Callanan, *Healy*, p. 685 n. 13.

[2] Press references in *Irish Independent*, 27–30 June 1919.

[3] NLI, Redmond Papers, MS 15209 (2): Murphy to O'Connor, 20 Dec. 1916.

[4] By-election poster in support of de Valera, 1917, indicating that Redmond was not an 'Irishman' because of his political views (see Mitchell and Ó Snodaigh (eds), *Irish Political Documents*, p. 34).

[5] McCartney, 'William Martin Murphy, Press Baron'.

SELECT BIBLIOGRAPHY

In addition to the William Martin Murphy Papers, made available by Gerald Murphy, the other main sources of information have been the minutes and reports of the Dublin Chamber of Commerce in the National Library of Ireland and the National Archives, Dublin; the Irish railway reports in the Railway Records Library and Archives at Heuston Station, Dublin; the letters to and from William Martin Murphy in the Archbishop Walsh Papers in the Dublin Diocesan Archives; the John Redmond Papers in the National Library; and the lectures/pamphlets by William Martin Murphy in Trinity College Library, Dublin, and in the National Library.

Contemporary newspapers and memoirs provided a rich store of information. The latter included T. M. Healy, *Letters and Leaders of My Day* (2 vols, London, 1928); T. P. O'Connor, *Memoirs of an Old Parliamentarian* (2 vols, London, 1929) and David Lloyd George, *War Memoirs* (2 vols, London, 1938 ed.).

Much assistance was also gained from a variety of biographies. These included F. S. L. Lyons, *Charles Stewart Parnell* (London, 1977) and *John Dillon* (London, 1968); Emmet Larkin, *James Larkin, Irish Labour Leader, 1876–1947* (London, 1989 ed.), Denis Gwynn, *The Life of John Redmond* (London, 1932), and Frank Callanan, *T. M. Healy* (Cork, 1996). For a specific event, Arnold Wright's *Disturbed Dublin: The Story of the Great Strike of 1913–14* (London, 1914) helped to set the scene.

Inevitably, numerous other sources were consulted, contemporary and otherwise. A number of these are mentioned in the Notes.

HISTORICAL ASSOCIATION OF IRELAND

Life and Times Series

●

'The Historical Association of Ireland is to be congratulated for its **Life and Times** Series of biographies. They are written in an authoritative, accessible and enjoyable way'

History Ireland

'Promises to be an important and valuable series'

Irish Historical Studies

'A very useful series and much to be welcomed by teachers'

Stair

●

No. 1 — HENRY GRATTAN
by JAMES KELLY

'The series has set a rigorous standard with this short study'

Books Ireland

'An up-to-date and sane account of the main aspects of Grattan's career'

K. Theodore Hoppen, Irish Historical Studies

No. 2 — SIR EDWARD CARSON
by ALVIN JACKSON

'A scintillating essay in reappraisal'

K. Theodore Hoppen, Irish Historical Studies

'Jackson's splendid *Sir Edward Carson*'

Irish Times

No. 3 — EAMON DE VALERA
by PAURIC TRAVERS

'A good short summary of a very long political life'

Stair